OLDHAM ATHLETIC

A PICTORIAL HISTORY

OLDHAM ATHLETIC

A PICTORIAL HISTORY

TONY BUGBY
INTRODUCTION BY JOE ROYLE

AMBERLEY

First published 2014

Amberley Publishing
The Hill, Stroud
Gloucestershire, GL5 4EP

www.amberley-books.com

British Library Cataloguing in Publication Data.
A catalogue record for this book is available from the British Library.

ISBN 978 1 4456 3861 4 (print)
ISBN 978 1 4456 3878 2 (ebook)

Typesetting by Amberley Publishing
Printed in the UK.

CONTENTS

PREFACE

Oldham Athletic's history has spanned three centuries and has certainly been an eventful and, at times, emotional roller coaster. Fans certainly cannot be labelled glory hunters, as Latics have managed to win only three championships since being formed in 1895. The title triumphs of 1952/53, 1973/74 and 1990/91 are etched in the minds of supporters, as were the halcyon days of more recent times under Joe Royle. They began with the 'pinch-me season' of 1989/90, when Latics reached Wembley in the Littlewood Cup (the one and only major final the club has ever reached), the semi-finals of the FA Cup and narrowly missed out on promotion. Latics captured the hearts of the nation as the team from the second tier of English football who defeated reigning League champions Arsenal and a host of other First Division teams in the cup competitions.

This was followed the next season by Royle guiding Latics back to the top division after an absence of sixty-eight years. The team spent three seasons among football's elite and in 1992, became founder members of the Premier League and they were assured of another place in history.

These magical moments were even sweeter bearing in mind the adversity the club has had to deal with. There were dark days as the club sought re-election to the Football League when its existence as one of the ninety-two came under serious threat.

Financial strife has also been a recurring problem, with 2003/04 a nightmare when the club's existence was under threat as it was forced into administration, a legacy of the disastrous ownership of later disgraced businessman Chris Moore. There was a serious threat the club might have ceased to exist until Simon Blitz, Danny Gazal and Simon Corney, three New York-based businessmen, completed their takeover.

Today, it remains a struggle financially due to dwindling attendances, and Mr Corney, the only one of the Three Amigos still involved in the football side, making no secret of his desire to sell.

INTRODUCTION

Joe Royle was Latics' manager for the most successful chapter in the club's history, which put the town well and truly on the footballing map. Here Royle gives his reflections on the glory days.

The twelve fantastic years I managed Latics provided memories which will stay with me forever. And the 1989/90 season is one which will never be forgotten as Second Division Latics claimed the scalps of the likes of Arsenal, Aston Villa and Everton. I remember going out for a drink in a local pub during those amazing Cup runs and a fan came up to me and told me he had to pinch himself to believe what was happening. That is how it became known as the 'pinch-me season'.

One of my abiding memories was arriving at Boundary Park one morning to discover three different queues – for the League Cup, FA Cup and a League fixture. And they were heading in different directions down Sheepfoot Lane.

And there was a unique spirit and such a special bond within the Oldham family. I still keep in touch with the likes of Mike Milligan, Rick Holden, Neil Adams, Frank Bunn and Andy Rhodes.

The players certainly enjoyed themselves. I often remarked I never knew where they were on a Wednesday (they frequently went out on Tuesday night as Wednesday was their day off) but I certainly knew where they were on a Saturday.

There is a saying that sometimes things happen for a reason and I may never have become Latics' manager as John Wile, the former West Brom centre-half, had initially been offered the job ahead of me.

Apparently he wanted his own staff and trimmings at a time when the club was close to bankruptcy and he turned it down.

I had just finished playing at Norwich due to a knee injury and was on their end-of-season to Montego Bay, Jamaica, when I saw an old newspaper with a report that Jimmy Frizzell had lost his job and the club was looking for a player-manager.

I applied on the off chance knowing my playing career was over but saying how much I admired the coaching and philosophies of the late Bill Taylor who had been at Latics and with whom I had worked at Manchester City.

Apparently it was well received, and I was invited for an interview and later called back for a second one when the story famously went that I arrived at Boundary Park on the back of a lorry.

I was, in fact, inside the lorry as the engine of my car had blown up not far from the ground, and I was hitching a lift when I was picked up by a Scouse lorry driver.

It was a great job as I inherited a good side which included players like Kenny Clements, Paul Futcher, Roger Palmer and Darron McDonough while Paul Atkinson and John Ryan were emerging.

We had to sell to survive in those days, but still progressed year by year, eventually building a side which brought us so much success.

I always maintained our best performance was the 3-3 draw against Manchester United in the 1990 semi-final of the FA Cup at Maine Road.

Our team had size, pace and ability, and was tailored to playing on the plastic pitch. So to go toe-to-toe with United on grass and be aggrieved that we didn't win was a great statement.

I was very proud to become the first manager to take Latics to a major Cup final and that season we so nearly made it to the final of the FA Cup.

We became Second Division champions the next season, and winning the title on the last day against Sheffield Wednesday was a great moment.

We were also founder members of the Premier League and then there was the great escape in 1992/93, when we had to win our last three games and also rely on Crystal Palace slipping to stay up. When we went to Villa, who still had a shout for the title, people had us down and we won 1-0, a victory which gave United their first title in twenty-six years.

We still had to beat Liverpool and Southampton and it was a terrific week and another of the magical times we had at Boundary Park.

Joe Royle

ACKNOWLEDGEMENTS

Special thanks to Joe Royle for writing the introduction, and also to Stewart Beckett for the loan of images from his huge personal archive. A big thank you also for the help and support from Dave Whaley, managing director at *Oldham Evening Chronicle*, and chief photographer Vincent Brown. Thank you to Oldham Athletic club photographers Tom Pickles and Alan Howarth, for providing photographs from more recent times. Finally, thanks to Jane Barlow for the many hours spent scanning and editing the pictures.

START OF THE JOURNEY

The remarkable journey began back in 1895, when Queen Victoria, Britain's longest-serving monarch, was still on the throne. Many of the country's professional clubs had the humblest of beginnings, a contrast to the illustrious histories they have since enjoyed. Manchester United, for example, was formed by employees of the Lancashire & Yorkshire Railway Company at their depot in Newton Heath. It was a similar story for the club that would eventually become Oldham Athletic, as it was probably formed over a pint at a local club.

John Goddard, the licensee of the Featherstall & Junction Inn, is the man credited with being the founder of the club in 1895, though there is no documentary evidence as to the precise date of the birth of Pine Villa. It was the love of the beautiful game that prompted Goddard (not Gartland as is commonly stated) and his son Fred to form a football team.

Goddard's friendship with officials from Oldham County, the town's professional team at that time, enabled him to strike a deal for the newly formed Pine Villa to ground share at Hudson Fold, where they played on alternate Saturdays. It was in the shadow of nearby Pine Mill that the club took its first tentative steps on a journey which has evolved over 119 years, although the groundsharing quickly ended after County formed a second team.

After two seasons of friendly fixtures when Berry's Field, Chadderton, was their home ground, Pine Villa's first campaign of competitive football was in 1897/98, when they were elected to Oldham Junior Association, Division Two. It was to be the start of a remarkable rise, as ten years later the club, which had evolved to become Oldham Athletic, were elected as members of the Football League.

Villa's debut season in local football was a memorable one, as the team won twelve of its fourteen League fixtures to be crowned champions and also win promotion. There was further success in 1898/99 as Villa, who moved to yet another new ground at Shiloh, finished runners-up in Division One to Greenacres Lads, the team they pipped to the title the previous season by one point. This time they lost out by the same margin, having lost only two of their sixteen League matches.

A committee meeting at the Black Cow Inn in July 1899, held primarily to decide what league to join, was to prove pivotal in the club's history. Oldham County had ceased to exist and George Elliott, one of the club's liquidators, suggested Villa make use of their old ground on Sheepfoot Lane. As this land was called Athletic Grounds, it seemed logical to have a name change, which is how Villa became Oldham Athletic.

There was not only a new name but a new league, as Oldham Athletic accepted an invitation to join the Manchester & District Alliance, a higher grade of football. The first

WHERE THE JOURNEY BEGAN: The Featherstall & Junction Inn where licensee John Goddard formed a football team called Pine Villa, which soon became OIdham Athletic.

game as Oldham Athletic came at the Athletic Grounds against Berry's Blacking Works, a team of shoemakers from Manchester, which they won 1-0 in front of a 1,000 crowd.

The first competitive fixture at Oldham Athletic came on Saturday 9 September 1899, when they defeated Failsworth club Nook Rovers 4-2 at the Athletic Grounds. This turned out to be another successful season as they finished third and also reached the final of the Manchester Alliance Cup, losing 3-1 to Failsworth Springhead.

There was no shortage of ambition as the club applied to join the semi-professional Manchester League for the 1900/01 season. They were subsequently elected along with Hyde and Northwich Victoria. After three successful seasons, Latics found it a difficult transition as they finished eleventh with only four teams beneath them in the table. There was also the upheaval of a change of home ground midseason after a dispute with landlords J. W. Lees Brewery over rent as they returned to their former home at Hudson Fold.

It was a case of strengthening the team and building slowly as Latics finished sixth, fourth and third in the three subsequent seasons in the Manchester League. They also won their first piece of silverware, lifting the Manchester Junior Cup.

The 1903/04 season was a success, with Latics finishing third, but Hudson Fold was closed for six weeks by the Football Association following crowd trouble after a 3-0 home defeat by Tonge FC when the referee was attacked at the end of the game.

Latics had earlier turned down an invitation in 1902 to join the Lancashire League, as club officials were mindful of what had happened to Oldham County five years earlier, and they were hoping to be on a sounder financial footing the next year. It would be two years before Latics left the Manchester League and joined the Lancashire Combination, though some at the club had more lofty ambitions.

At one stage in 1904, they decided to apply for election to the second division of the Football League, though a new committee later quashed that proposal and instead opted to apply for election to Division B of the Lancashire Combination. There were no half measures as ambitious Latics brought in ten new players, intending to become a force in their new league. They included former Liverpool, Preston and England international Frank Becton, though he mysteriously disappeared after only one match for his new club.

This was another successful season, as they won promotion having finished third. There were some landslide victories, including an 11-0 success against Newton-le-Willows, their biggest win to date. Despite further strengthening of the team, the debut campaign in division one of the Lancashire Combination only proved moderately successful as they finished thirteenth in the twenty-team League. This was despite making marquee signings such as Alexander McAllister, a former championship winner for Sunderland, from Derby County, and James Hodson, who had been in Bury's squad when they won the FA Cup two years earlier.

The opposition was stronger than any previously encountered, as it included the reserve sides from Manchester United, Manchester City, Liverpool, Everton, Bolton, Blackburn Rovers and Preston North End, while the winners were Accrington Stanley.

Latics also broke new ground this season by entering the FA Cup for the first time. They defeated Ashton Town, Fairfield and Stalybridge Rovers before drawing Football League club Hull City in the first round proper, narrowly losing 2-1. It was becoming increasingly obvious that Latics were destined for League football sooner rather than later.

In April 1906, four momentous decisions were made: the club became a limited company, with a capital of £2,000 divided into 4,000 shares of 10s; an application was made to join the second division of the Football League; a first-ever team manager was appointed; and attempts were made to secure a lease to return to Boundary Park after a six-year absence, with a seven-year agreement subsequently reached with brewers J. W. Lees.

David Ashworth's appointment as the club's first secretary-manager coincided with Latics' return to Boundary Park from Hudson Fold. Within four years of the former referee taking charge, he had guided Latics from the Lancashire Combination to the First Division of the Football League. Ashworth was usually seen sporting a bowler hat, and he also had a waxed moustache. However, his stern appearance disguised a sense of humour, for he was said to style his moustache with both ends up after a win, both ends down after a defeat, and one up and one down after a draw.

Latics had failed by one vote in 1906 to gain a place in the League as Chesterfield Town, Burton United and Clapton Orient were all re-elected, so faced another season in the Combination. Ashworth wasted no time bringing in five new players inside his first working week and a further five the following week as there was a major overhaul of the playing squad. The first of the signings, Henry Hancock, recruited from Blackpool, would prove to be among the best of Latics' early inside-forwards.

MOUSTACHE: Latics' first-ever manager David Ashworth with his famous waxed moustache, which he used to turn up or down depending on whether his team had won or lost.

The changes were a resounding success as Latics went from finishing thirteenth the previous season to finishing champions and scoring close to 150 goals in all competitions.

There was also an exciting FA Cup run, which saw Latics finally knocked out in the second round proper by Liverpool, who won 1-0 at Boundary Park in front of a crowd of 21,538 with gate receipts of £619 12s 9d.

It looked as though Latics were set to lose out for a second successive year in their pursuit of a place in the Football League. Lincoln City and Chesterfield Town retained their League status in 1907, while non-League Fulham replaced Burton. The directors of Latics, one of six non-League clubs to apply for election, decided to immediately apply to join the Southern League in place of Fulham.

However, Bradford Park Avenue's directors had done the same and it was the Yorkshire club that was successful; Latics seemed set to stay in the Combination for a third season.

Latics' luck changed in early June, when Burslem Port Vale was forced to resign from the Football League's Second Division through financial difficulties. They immediately applied to fill the vacancy, as did Burton United and Rotherham Town, but it was Latics who were unanimously elected at an emergency meeting of the League in Blackpool.

Ashworth had less than three months to build a squad in readiness for the start of a new and exciting chapter in the club's short history. He brought in six players: full-back James Hamilton and inside-forward William Dodds from Burslem Port Vale, goalkeeper Robert Hewitson (Crystal Palace), outside-right John Hesham (Leyton), centre-half John Shufflebotham (Small Heath) and centre-forward Frank Newton (Bradford City).

LATICS WIN FOOTBALL LEAGUE STATUS

The historic first match as a League club was on Saturday 7 September at Stoke City, which represented a formidable challenge as they had been a First Division side for most of their existence. Latics were not fazed and emerged 3-1 winners, with Dodds having the distinction of scoring their first-ever League goal. Newton scored a total of thirty-four League and Cup goals that campaign, and Jim Swarbrick also found the net that day.

West Bromwich Albion were the first visitors to Boundary Park the following Saturday, when a crowd of 17,000 saw Latics triumph 2-1. The match was refereed by Herbert Bamlett, who would become Latics' manager in 1914.

Latics certainly acquitted themselves well, as they finished third behind Bradford City and Leicester Fosse. They narrowly missed out on becoming the first club in history to win promotion to the First Division after only one season of League football.

The promotion places were not determined until the last day of the season, when Latics were held to a goalless draw at Glossop North End, while Leicester beat Stoke to clinch second spot. Home gates almost doubled to an average of 10,270 as the club reported a profit for the year at its annual general meeting.

While a largely successful season, there was one blemish. Thus came following an ill-tempered 3-3 draw in February at home to Fulham, the club that had been elected to the Football League ahead of them ten months earlier. The referee, who had made a number of questionable decisions, had to be escorted from the field by a police constable, and it was alleged goalkeeper Hewitson had thrown a missile at the match official. The Fulham coach was stoned as it left the ground with windows shattered, leaving the players and officials badly shaken.

The Football Association launched an inquiry and Latics were found guilty of misconduct and fined £10, while Hewitson was convicted of throwing mud at the referee and of inciting a riot. He was banned for fourteen days and that summer joined newly elected League club Tottenham Hotspur.

Latics' disappointment at missing out on promotion by only two points was compensated for they won the Lancashire Cup, beating Preston North End 2-0 in the final at Hyde Road, home of Manchester City.

Ashworth continued his team building for 1908/09 by signing forwards Finlay Speedie and William Appleyard from Newcastle, and full-back William Cope and outside-right

OPENER: A team shot from 1907/08, Latics' first season as a Football League club.

ACTION: A rare photograph from Latics' second home game as a Football League club against Hull City in September 1907.

Arthur Griffiths from Stoke City for a joint fee of £300; Stoke City resigned from the League shortly before the new season began due to financial problems. There was also a new goalkeeper as Howarth Matthews arrived from Burton United. He would become one of the all-time greats as he served the club for eighteen years and made 344 appearances. Ashworth also brought in Scottish wing-half James Reid and inside-forward William Andrews from Northern Ireland club Glentoran on the eve of the new campaign.

The second campaign failed to match the exploits of the opener. It soon became apparent they would not be able to sustain another push for promotion, and they finished sixth.

Ashworth made one notable signing midseason as Scottish outside-left Joe Donnachie was signed from Everton for £250. He went on to serve the club with distinction for the next eight years.

When Latics failed to win in their first five League games of the 1909/10 season, which yielded only two points, there was a mood of despair and despondency hanging over the club. Latics were languishing at the bottom of the table in mid-October when Ashworth signed wing-half Alex Downie from Manchester United for £600 and inside-forward Bill Montgomery from Sunderland for a fee of £350.

Downie was made captain and Montgomery scored sixteen goals in twenty-eight appearances as the pair helped transform Latics' fortunes. By the New Year, Latics had seven wins, seven losses and threes draw as they had climbed to midtable. There was still no inking, however, as to what lay ahead in a remarkable second half to the season. Latics produced a remarkable run, which saw them lose only once in twenty-one League fixtures to finish second and clinch promotion. They went into the last game in third place, two points behind Hull, who were second, and who visited Boundary Park in a winner-takes-all clash.

Hull knew a draw would be enough to clinch promotion, while Latics, who had a vastly superior goal difference, were aware a win may not be enough, as Derby would finish the season with one more point than Latics if they beat West Brom. Latics did their job, soundly beating Hull 3-0 in front of a crowd of 29,083, while secretary Bob Mellor, who served the club for forty-three years, had to wait for a telephone call that Derby had been held to a goalless draw at West Brom.

Only one point separated the top four clubs, and Latics finished runners-up ahead of Hull and Derby on goal difference. The goals of half-back Jimmy Fay, pressed into action as an emergency inside forward in the promotion campaign, certainly proved decisive as he found the net twenty-six times in thirty-eight League appearances. There was also a key contribution from Alf Toward, a December signing from Hull, who scored thirteen times in twenty-one League appearances.

The concern as the 1910/11 season approached was whether a club like Latics, still in its infancy, could compete with the game's elite, as it was regarded as a footballing fairytale how a club, only in its fourth season in the Football League, had reached such heights.

Ashworth retained almost all the players who had helped the club win promotion, but strengthened the side with some notable additions as they signed goalkeeper Hugh McDonald (Woolwich Arsenal), Scottish international inside-forward John McTavish (Falkirk) and wing-half Alec Wilson (Preston North End). Then, early in the campaign, they bought winger George Woodger from Crystal Palace for £750. Interest was such that the number of 'guinea' season tickets sold increased from 300 to 500.

Latics kicked off their First Division campaign with a creditable 1-1 draw at Aston Villa, who would go on to finish the season as runners-up. It provided evidence that they would not be out of their depth. The historic first home League match saw 34,000 pack into Boundary Park for the visit of Newcastle United, who spoilt the party as they left 2-0 victors.

It would prove a season of consolidation, though there were some notable successes. Latics completed League doubles over Sunderland, who finished third, and also against Sheffield United as they finished a respectable seventh. Latics found goalscoring far more challenging in the First Division; they found the net forty-four times as opposed to seventy-nine the previous season in the second tier. Toward finished the leading marksman with twelve League goals.

Ashworth's stock was rising and Latics' delighted directors rewarded him with a three-year extension to his contract. Latics also broke new ground at the end of the 1910/11 season when they embarked upon their first excursion into Europe on a three-week, six-match tour to Budapest and Vienna, where they played for the Hungarian Cup and Anglo-Austrian Cup.

The second season in the top flight proved a more sobering experience, as Latics avoided relegation by the skin of their teeth. They finished third bottom, just one point clear of Preston, who were demoted.

The directors again backed Ashworth, who signed outside-right Tom Marrison from Nottingham Forest, while midseason centre-half George Hunter was bought from Aston Villa for £1,250, becoming the club's first four-figure signing. There was, however, one notable departure: Jimmy Fay left for Bolton Wanderers in a £750 deal following a disagreement over travelling expenses from his home in Southport. That meant the break-up of the reliable half-back line of Fay, Walders and Wilson.

Latics had no worries early in the campaign, but then the wheels came off in a two-month period from the end of October, when they won only once in twelve League matches. There was then an amazing turnabout in Latics' fortunes as they went unbeaten in twelve League matches from 1 January – the day Hunter made his debut – until Easter Monday. However, Latics were forced to endure a nerve-jangling finish to the season after picking up one point from their last four games to suddenly become embroiled in a battle to stay up.

Fans were fickle, even in those days, with directors voicing their concern about dwindling attendances. Latics had scored only ten goals in their final thirteen League matches, something that was addressed by Ashworth that summer as Welsh international forward Evan Jones, inside-forward Bill Montgomery and winger Tommy Broad were all released. They were replaced by inside-forward Joe Walters, a £900 signing from Aston Villa, Oliver Tummon, an outside-right from Gainsborough Trinity, and Welsh international centre-forward Walter Davies.

There was a marked upturn in Latics' fortunes in 1912/13, and at one stage they were challenging for a League and Cup double. They beat Bolton Wanderers, Nottingham Forest, Manchester United and Everton to reach the semi-final of the FA Cup, when they were beaten 1-0 by Everton at Ewood Park.

The sale of centre-half Hunter to Chelsea on 1 March was pinpointed by many as the moment the team went into declin, the last two months of the season yielding only three wins

CUP TIE: Action from Latics' FA Cup semi-final against Aston Villa, which was played at Blackburn Rovers' Ewood Park in 1913.

from their last twelve League matches as they slipped to a disappointing ninth place. A season that had promised so much ended on a flat note, though the final match of the season, a goalless draw against Manchester United, saw Ashworth hand a debut to amateur goalkeeper Ted Taylor. He would later become an England international and win championship medals for Huddersfield Town and Everton. Taylor, who had been signed from Liverpool Balmoral for £30, would later be sold to Huddersfield for a club record £1,950.

Ashworth's priorities for the 1913/14 season were to add a centre-half and centre-forward to his squad, believing he had the nucleus of a fine team. Latics broke their transfer record, splashing out £1,750 for Charlie Roberts, the Manchester United captain and England international, while striker Bill Douglas was brought in from Cardiff City as cover as Ashworth intended to persevere with Gilbert Kemp at centre-forward.

With a new grandstand (the present main stand) being constructed, Latics looked ahead with optimism, and that was borne out as they finished fourth, their highest placing in their four seasons in the First Division. However, there was a major blow financially following a first-round defeat in the FA Cup at Brighton as gates plummeted for the remainder of the season.

The Football League and Football Association decided the 1914/15 season should proceed despite the outbreak of the First World War and the fact that many players, including ones from Latics, had left to fight for their country. Ashworth also dropped a bombshell, resigning to take over as secretary-manager at Stockport County for a reportedly much larger salary. He was replaced by well-known referee Herbert Bamlett, who was one of sixty applicants for the job. Bamlett signed centre-forward Arthur Cashmore from Manchester United and full-back Harry Grundy on amateur forms from Little Lever Colliery.

Latics enjoyed their best season yet, finishing runners-up, though there was a disappointing finish to the campaign. They needed three points from the last two games, both at home, to be crowned champions. They were beaten by both Burnley and Liverpool and Everton won the title by a margin of one point.

Looking back, Latics' form had dipped in the second part of the season; they had reached the turn of the year having suffered only two League losses in nineteen games. They managed just one meagre win in January and February when the damage was inflicted.

Centre-forward Kemp, who established a regular place for the first time, enjoyed his most productive season, finishing top scorer with sixteen League goals, which included the club's only hat-trick of the season in a 6-2 home win against Bradford City. There were a further three goals in the FA Cup.

There had been earlier controversy when Latics' match at Middlesbrough over Easter was abandoned with thirty-one minutes left when full-back Billy Cook refused to leave the field after being sent off. Unsurprisingly, this caused uproar as never before had a game been abandoned. This was compounded when Cook played at Manchester City two days later before the Football League had decided what action to take. They were not amused

HIGHEST FINISH: The Latics team that finished runners-up in the First Division in 1914/15, when they were pipped for the title on the last day by Everton.

and Cook was suspended for one year. Latics were fined £300, severely reprimanded and the result was left to stand as Boro were 4-1 ahead at the time.

Hostilities meant official football was suspended at the end of the 1914/15 season at a time when Latics were enjoying their most successful spell. It left fans wondering just how good their team might have become.

The Football League organised regional competitions, and Latics were involved in the Lancashire Section for a period of four years. Each season, this involved a principal tournament on a League basis followed by a subsidiary, which had different formats as it entailed between six and ten additional games. Latics were still able to call upon a number of the regulars from peacetime football, including the likes of Charlie Roberts, Arthur Dixon, Jimmy Hodson, David Wilson, Joe Donnachie, Arthur Cashmore, Howard Matthews, Elliott Pilkington and Arthur Gee.

Latics were saddened in November 1915 to learn that outside-right Frank Hesham had been killed in action. They later lost two reserve team players, Jack Lane and George Perry. Others, like Finlay Speedie and William Bradbury, were awarded medals, while George Hunter rose to the rank of CMS and saw active service in France and Gallipoli. David Walders, meanwhile, was wounded in action, and would never play again.

However, as the war continued, it became increasingly difficult to field a settled side and there were occasions when secretary Robert Mellor was not able to finalise his side until minutes before kick-off. There were even times when playing away games that Latics had to call on the home club to provide players to make up a full complement.

POST-WAR BLUES

The end of the Great War enabled football to return to normal in 1919/20, though Latics found the heart had been ripped out of their successful side. There were the departures of Donnachie (Everton), Kemp (Bradford City) and James Broad (Millwall), coupled with the retirements of Roberts and Hodson.

It was a new-look team that included thirty-four-year-old outside-right George Wall, who was signed from Manchester United for £200. In his prime, he won the League title with the Reds in 1907/08, and FA Cup in 1909, as well as gaining seven full caps for England.

Latics endured a wretched start to their first post-war campaign, losing thirteen of their first twenty games with a lack of goals again an acute problem. Their fortunes changed with a run of three straight victories at the start of January, each by 1-0 margins as they defeated Chelsea at Boundary Park, followed by Newcastle United home and away.

The signing of Irish international forward Billy Halligan from Preston North End helped maintain the improvement. He scored twice on his debut in a 3-2 defeat at Arsenal in early February.

Gee scored match-winning goals in 1-0 victories against Blackburn Rovers and Sheffield Wednesday in the final three weeks of the season as Latics finished seventeenth from twenty-two clubs. They only escaped the drop by two points. Gee's contribution was immense as he finished leading marksman with thirteen League goals, the only player to reach double figures as they again toiled in front of goal.

Bamlett twice broke Latics' transfer record before the start of the 1920/21 season, splashing out £1,850 for Middlesbrough centre-forward Reuben Butler and £2,500 for Fulham half-back Alf Marshall. The spending increased to £8,020 during the season after the arrivals of inside-forward Jim Marshall (Bradford City), half-back Bill Taylor (Burnley) and inside-forward Tommy Byrom (Rochdale). Butler scored the winning goals in the opening two matches at his former club Middlesbrough and at home to Blackburn.

The early euphoria quickly evaporated as Latics went on their worst run as a League club. They recorded only one further win until mid-February, during which time they suffered twelve defeats and drew their remaining eleven games. Luckily for Latics, Butler, who had failed to find the net for almost four months, suddenly rediscovered his form as twelve of his eighteen goals came from February onwards. They proved the catalyst for Latics climbing out of the relegation places to finish nineteenth,seven points clear of the drop zone.

Bamlett resigned that close season to become manager of Wigan Borough for their first season in the new Third Division North, and old boy Charlie Roberts was appointed as his successor. His Royal Highness, The Prince of Wales paid a visit to Boundary Park in July 1921 to visit ex-serviceman and disabled soldiers from Oldham and 40,000 gathered inside the ground. Latics hoped the return of Roberts as manager would inspire in the same way he did as a player.

Sadly, it turned out to be another battle against relegation as they again finished in nineteenth place, though again there had been early promise when they put together a run of four straight victories.

Latics managed only a further four victories from early October to mid-March, during which time there was one spell when they failed to find the net in six successive games and the spectre of relegation again loomed large.

Once again, though, Latics pulled away from danger after a strong finish to the season, in which they recorded five wins and three draws from their last eleven League games. What made that run remarkable was that they beat the teams who would occupy the top three places: champions Liverpool, runners-up Tottenham and Burnley. The two other wins were against Newcastle and Aston Villa, who finished seventh and fifth respectively as Latics produced their best displays against the top teams to finish five points clear of the relegation places.

Roberts brought in half-back George Waddell from Preston for £250, outside-right and former England amateur international George Douglas, a £750 signing from Burnley, along with centre-forward Billy Hibbert, who cost £500 from Bradford City.

After three successive seasons of struggle, there would be no escape this time and Latics lost their First Division status in 1922/23. Remarkably, it would be sixty-eight years before they regained it. It was also the first relegation the club had suffered in its history. There had been no inkling as to what a disastrous campaign it would be, as Latics started brightly, winning three and drawing one of their first five fixtures.

BOUNDARY PARK: A shot from the early 1920s when Furtherwood Lane was still a cobbled street.

It then went horribly wrong as they managed to pick up two measly draws from nine League games to plummet down the table. There was also a spell in the same period when Latics failed to find the net in seven games from a spell of nine fixtures. And with the threat of relegation looming and reported problems behind the scenes, Roberts resigned as manager at Christmas 1922.

Latics' directors, remembering the good times under Ashworth, persuaded their former manager to return in January 1923. It was a coup for Latics, though a strange decision for Ashworth, as he was manager of Liverpool, who were top of the First Division and on course for a second successive League championship, which they duly achieved later in the campaign. Ashworth, who had been tempted by a lucrative deal, believed the key to survival was signing two top strikers, but with Latics strapped for cash due to dwindling gates, it was impossible. Latics lost seven League games in a row in December/January, scoring only three goals and conceding sixteen.

Back-to-back wins against Birmingham City (in those days clubs usually played each other on successive weekends) gave Latics a flicker of hope they might survive. It proved a false dawn as Latics won only three of their last thirteen League games to finish bottom of the table. Despite a disastrous campaign, though, they were only four points from safety. The Achilles heel was a lack of firepoweR; they managed to score only thirty-five goals in forty-two League games, with Scottish striker Jim Marshall their leading marksman with six.

Fans were so disillusioned that they voted with their feet and stayed away. Their last game in the top flight against Cardiff City attracted a crowd of only 4,051 at Boundary Park, whereas one month earlier there had been a gate of 19,149 for the home game against Newcastle. Ironically, Latics signed off with a 3-1 win against the Bluebirds, and little did anybody realise how long it would before they again played at the highest level of English football.

Ashworth set about rebuilding the side. He captured half-back Tom Heaton and inside-forward Archie Longmuir from Blackburn Rovers, Bradford City's inside-forward Bill Howson and Thomas Fleetwood, a half-back who had earlier won the League title with Everton. They helped offset the departures, the most notable of which was Reginald Freeman, the full-back being transferred to Middlesbrough for the considerable sum of £4,000.

The high volume of season tickets sold showed optimism that Latics could quickly regain their top-flight status. However, only two wins from their first twelve League games brought about a realisation that Latics would be remaining in the Second Division. The club finally rediscovered their form, and between November and March rekindled promotion hopes following a run of only two defeats in twenty League games.

That coincided with centre-forward John Blair, an amateur, breaking into a team that had again been starved of goals. He made his debut on New Year's Day and became top scorer with fifteen League and Cup goals in only nineteen appearances. It prompted a remark from former Latics' player Billy Cook that, with full-time training, he would be one of the best centre-forwards in the land. Sadly, he fractured his ankle the next season and that promise and potential was never realised. Latics ran out of steam, losing their last three games and winning only one of their final eight League fixtures to finish seventh, yet only six points shy of second-placed Bury.

RELEGATION: The team that was relegated from the First Division in 1923. It would take sixty-eight years for Latics to regain their top-flight

In that season, Latics were also involved in a bizarre game in which full-back Sam Wynne scored two goals and also two own goals in a 3-2 win against Manchester United at Boundary Park. Sadly, he died later aged just thirty when playing for Bury. He collapsed taking a free-kick and died in the changing room.

There were upheavals in the summer of 1924 as Latics, even then saddled by large debts, were forced to release prized assets such as inside-forward Frank Hargreaves, who was sold to Everton for £750. Preparations for the new campaign were disrupted further when Ashworth left to become Manchester City manager. He apparently had an escape clause in his contract that permitted him to leave if a 'better post' became available. Bob Mellor succeeded Ashworth, one of three separate spells he had as manager between 1924 and 1945, as he also combined the job with being club secretary.

It was a tough start, as Latics' directors had to guarantee overdrafts at the bank as well as find money from their own pockets. Chairman L. R. Stanton also sounded ominous, warning that if gates didn't improve something very serious might happen to the club.

It was against this bleak backdrop that Latics opened the campaign with only nineteen professionals, and three of them were injured for the kick-off. They were forced to sign up a number of local amateur players to make up their numbers.

Latics began with a promising goalless draw at Southampton before the stark reality of their problems became clear, losing 5-1 at Clapton Orient and 5-0 at home to Chelsea in their next two games. Then, in the fourth game, a 2-1 home victory against Orient, Blair broke his ankle. The season became a bitter struggle to avoid relegation to Third Division North.

Latics' fate was determined on the last day of the season, when they beat Crystal Palace 1-0 thanks to a John Keedwell goal to stay up, following a winner-takes-all clash that saw the Londoners demoted to the Third Division. As we will discover later, this would be the first of many last-day dramas when Latics would experience either the joy of a great escape or heartbreak of relegation.

Finances were so dire there was a threat the club would go under, until the *Oldham Evening Chronicle*'s *Green Final* sports paper launched a public appeal, which raised over £4,000, clearing debts and paying the summer wages.

Interestingly, that summer Latics were given the opportunity to sign two promising Durham City players for a combined fee of £750. The minutes from a board meeting resolved that directors could not sanction such expenditure. One of the players was George Camsell, who signed for Middlesbrough, for whom he scored fifty-nine goals in their Second Division title-winning campaign two years later.

After averting financial meltdown, Latics began the 1925/26 season with renewed vigour, brought about by an array of new signings, including Billy Goodwin (Crewe), Charlie Hey (Hurst), Horace Barnes (Preston), Ted Goodier (Lancaster Town), Albert Pynegar (Coventry City) and Arthur Ormston (Wigan Borough), while Hargreaves returned from Everton. The goals from Ormston, who scored five in a 7-2 win against Stoke, and Pynegar helped Latics sustain an early push for promotion.

Three straight defeats over Christmas heralded a slide, and their form in the second half of the season was decidedly patchy, though they finished the campaign in a respectable seventh spot. They concluded the campaign with an 8-3 home win against Nottingham Forest, their record margin of victory in the League up to that point. They had, however, earlier in the campaign done even better, defeating Lytham 10-1 in the preliminary round of the FA Cup as they rediscovered the art of goalscoring.

Ormston, bought from Wigan Borough for just £25, top scored with twenty-three League and Cup goals, while Bert Watson finished with nineteen and Pynegar sixteen. Long-serving goalkeeper Howard Matthews left in the summer of 1926 after eighteen years and 344

MATCH-DAY TRAFFIC: The scene on match day back in the early 1920s.

appearances, while the injury-plagued Blair also moved, transferring his amateur status to Arsenal.

The calibre of the players recruited by Mellor that summer was regarded as a higher standard to the challenging previous couple of years. This optimism was only heightened as Latics won their first three games of the season, each by a 1-0 margin. Latics won seven and drew one of their first eleven matches, and average home attendances rose to almost 16,000.

The early season promise evaporated with the onset of winter, though they finished the campaign strongly, with five wins and two draws from their last seven League games to claim tenth place.

Pynegar finished top scorer with nineteen League and Cup goals, but during the season there were three notable departures: Welsh international 'keeper Bert Gray to Manchester City for £2,250; Wynne to Bury for the same sum; and Ormston, the previous year's top scorer, to Bradford City for £650. Wynne sadly died during a game for Bury against Sheffield United only four months after leaving Boundary Park, and before Latics' last game of the season at home to South Shields there was one minute's silence while a band played 'Abide With Me'. It was an emotional day and a collection at Boundary Park that afternoon raised almost £30 for Wynne's widow.

Latics had a new manager for the 1927/28 season following the appointment of Andrew Wilson, the elder brother of former player David, who stands fourth in the club's all-time appearance list, having played 397 games for the club. Wilson came with an impressive playing pedigree, having won title First Division titles and the FA Cup for Sheffield Wednesday, for whom he made over 500 appearances. He also won six caps for Scotland.

Ironically, when Latics played Sheffield Wednesday at Boundary Park on Christmas Eve 1910, the brothers had been captains of the respective teams. Andrew Wilson had cut his managerial teeth at Bristol Rovers, where he spent five years before joining Latics, vowing to return them to the First Division.

His first signing was former Scottish international inside-forward Neil Harris, who cost £400 from Newcastle United, where he was a member of their FA Cup-winning team of 1924. Harris was one of eight new signings as Latics kicked off the campaign with a playing staff of thirty, making it difficult to field a settled side.

It looked as though Latics would be able to mount a push for promotion until the third week in February, when their season fell apart; they managed only four wins and two draws from their final fourteen League games to finish seventh. Pynegar was again top scorer with nineteen for the second successive season, and he was one of four players to reach double figures.

Wilson's first season as manager was tainted by controversy when Fulham claimed that Latics' director, Arthur Barlow, had offered to throw the League game at Craven Cottage in return for their winning bonus being paid to Latics' players. Mr Barlow was found guilty by the Football Association and received a life ban from football management. The ban was lifted six years later and he returned to the board at Boundary Park, eventually becoming chairman.

During the campaign, there were problems as the roof of the Chaddy End twice blew off due to winds, which were described as hurricane-like in strength. Wilson brought in six new players for the 1928/29 campaign, including Tom Smelt and Cliff Foster from

Manchester City. Latics, hit by injuries, made a disastrous start to the season, losing nine of their opening ten League games, the lone victory at home to Reading.

Indeed, Latics reached Christmas with only eight points from their first nineteen League fixtures, and relegation looked a certainty. Latics produced a great escape as they won thirteen of their twenty-three League matches between Christmas and the end of the season to escape relegation by just three points.

Stewart Littlewood, a £1,300 signing from Port Vale in January 1929, was leading scorer with twelve goals as he helped inspire the revival. The upturn in fortunes coincided with Wilson giving young players their chance, including the likes of Fred Worrall, Jimmy Dyson, Matt Gray and Bill Hasson. Latics had lost Naylor midseason and he was transferred to Huddersfield Town for what was then a club record £3,750.

The 1929/30 season saw Latics come as close to regaining their top-flight status as at any time in the sixty-eight years they took to finally achieve it. Wilson brought in five new players including Seth King, a £400 capture from Sheffield United, who was also appointed club captain.

What a contrast to the dismal start to the previous campaign, as Latics lost only one of their first fifteen League games. They were top of the table for much of the campaign and five points clear at the three-quarter stage, but they slipped up late on to finish third, missing out on promotion by only two points. This was down to a failure to win any of their last five games, when they were hit by injuries to key players.

Latics were still able to reflect on a remarkable season in which they scored ninety goals in their forty-two League fixtures. Littlewood finished with twenty-eight in League and Cup, while Gray also hit twenty. There was also an epic FA Cup fourth-round tie against First Division champions Sheffield Wednesday, who won 4-3 at Boundary Park in front of a record crowd of 46,471. It was described as the finest game staged on the ground.

Latics did not appear to be suffering a hangover from the disappointing finish to the previous season, winning four of their first five fixtures in 1930/31. However, this turned out to be false optimism as the season fell away and they finished a disappointing twelfth – though a 35 per cent drop in attendances was of more concern and the season was described as a financial disaster.

The *Green Final* newspaper reported that fans would stay away from Boundary Park unless the team was battling for promotion or playing like Arsenal, who were that era's purveyors of fine football. The disappointment was compounded by Third Division (South) side Watford winning 3-1 at Boundary Park in their only FA Cup game as the possibility of a lucrative Cup run also rapidly vanished.

Latics, who scored for fun the previous season, managed only sixteen in twenty-one away League games. Littlewood, top scorer for each of the two previous seasons, suffered a marked loss of form and was transferred back to Port Vale in March 1931 for £1,550. Jimmy Dyson finished top marksman with sixteen goals.

Latics, still beset by money worries, upset fans by increasing the price of season tickets for 1931/32 by 25 per cent to £3. They then proceeding to have a wretched season in which they finished eighteenth and avoided relegation by only three points after securing late wins against Bradford Park Avenue and Charlton Athletic. The nineteen League losses included a 7-1 defeat at Wolves, while they also shipped five goals on five further occasions.

SHOT
STOPPER:
Latics' 'keeper
Jack Hacking
makes a save
against Chelsea
at Stamford
Bridge in 1930.

It was hardly surprising that the team toiled because there had been an exodus of top players to bring in much-needed revenue. Goalkeeper Frank Moss, who bizarrely had been rushed to hospital after swallowing his teeth in a pre-season game, was sold to Arsenal for £2,225 early in the campaign. Moss was followed midseason by Fred Worrall to Portsmouth for £3,000, Ted Goodier and Les Adlam to QPR for a joint fee of £1,500 and Jimmy Dyson to Grimsby Town for £2,350, leaving the squad threadbare.

William Johnstone, who had been signed from Arsenal in January 1931 for £2,130, and John Pears were joint top scorers with eleven goals, while Teddy Ivill was an ever present for a fifth successive season. With attendances again a major cause for concern, the one bright spot was the FA Cup tie against Huddersfield Town, which attracted a gate of 30,607, producing receipts of £1,903, when the average figure for the last eight games had been £230. Manager Wilson, frustrated by the financial constraints, left to join Stockport County in July 1932 and club secretary Mellor again took charge.

Only four players from the side which finished third in the 1929/30 campaign remained for the start of 1932/33, though, in fairness, Latics did invest a small amount of the cash raised from sales. Mellor brought in seven players and spent a modest £300 on Manchester United inside-forward Billy Johnston and £200 for Accrington Stanley outside-right Alf Agar. Latics' directors turned down the chance to introduce potentially lucrative greyhound racing to Boundary Park, which pleased church leaders.

The 1932/33 season developed into another scrap against relegation, and the club was engulfed by another financial crisis. There was a serious risk of Latics folding after the bank put the brake on lending, and the directors were again forced to dig deep to help the club financially. Latics badly needed to strengthen and Manchester City came to their aid in mid-February, loaning forward Harry Rowley and former player Jimmy Naylor, while not long after Manchester United sent them centre-forward Tommy Reid.

The temporary signings proved the turning point of the campaign because, after a run of eight straight losses, they posted four straight wins to ease their troubles. Latics, in fact, won eight and drew two of their last thirteen League games as they climbed to sixteenth place and four points clear of the relegation places. John Pears was again top scorer, this time with thirteen goals while, significantly, Reid weighed in with nine from only thirteen appearances following his March move from Old Trafford.

There was another mid-season high-profile departure as Ivill was sold to Charlton Athletic for £1,700, and his incredible run of playing 224 consecutive games ended. Mellor reverted to being club secretary when former Scottish international and Manchester City player Jimmy McMullan was appointed manager in May 1933.

There was a spirit of optimism going into McMullan's opening campaign, and they managed to keep together the nucleus of the side that had finished the previous season strongly. That included signing Rowley and Reid on a permanent basis for £750 and £400 respectively. The season saw Latics' fortunes improve markedly as they finished ninth and, opposed to looking beneath them, they actually briefly flirted with the prospect of promotion. Reid repaid his fee by finishing top scorer with seventeen goals.

What made finishing ninth even more creditable was that there were further sales during the season: Clifton Chadwick (Middlesbrough), Pears (Preston) and Jack Hacking (Manchester United). The FA Cup also provided a much-needed cash windfall as a home fourth-round tie against Sheffield Wednesday attracted a crowd of 46,011. Latics drew 1-1 only to lose the replay 6-1 in front of another bumper attendance of 41,311.

Apart from the Cup ties, only one League game produced receipts exceeding £1,000, and that was for the visit of Manchester United when the crowd was 22,520. By contrast, the last home game against Hull City attracted a paltry 2,986 and receipts of just £83. The stay-away fans missed a treat as Latics triumphed 7-0. Earlier derbies against Bolton and Blackpool attracted crowds of less than 10,000, prompting a newspaper report to state the game was dead in the town.

CLASS OF 1932/33: Back row (from left): Bob Grice, Billy Porter, Bill Naylor. Front: Alf Agar, John Pears, Joe Brunskill, Jack Hacking.

Manager McMullan stunned the club by resigning after only twelve months to become Aston Villa's first-ever team manager. Club secretary Mellor was again summoned to take charge of the team. This would be his longest spell, as he remained in charge until February 1945. The financial troubles continued with the much-abused directors again paying the summer wages, while the popular Hasson was transferred to Millwall.

Mellor managed to bring in six new players for the 1934/35 season, but it was evident early on that the team was not good enough. Sadly, there were no funds to strengthen the side and it would prove to be the most calamitous campaign in the club's history, as they were relegated to the third tier of English football for the first time.

They won only five of their first eighteen League matches before a run of eight straight losses effectively sealed their fate; they finished second bottom to Notts County and six points from safety. During the season there were further departures as Rowley and Billy Porter were both sold to Manchester United for £1,375 and £2,000 respectively. Inside-forward Bill Walsh, signed from Fleetwood for £125 in November 1933, was top scorer with twelve goals, while the main problems were defensive; they leaked ninety-five League goals, the highest number since gaining Football League status.

There was a new-look squad for the start of the 1935/36 season and the start of a new adventure in Division Three North. Mellor brought in fourteen new players, including Bolton Wanderers' inside-forward Bill Chambers in an exchange deal involving popular goalkeeper Fred Swift, the brother of Manchester City legend Frank.

The early season optimism quickly disappeared as Latics discovered that the division was tougher than envisaged. Latics' form was patchy, as proved by events over the festive period. They defeated Tranmere Rovers 4-1 at Boundary Park on Christmas Day, only to

CUP CLASH: Billy Johnstone and Tottenham's Arthur Rowe challenge for the ball during Latics' 6-0 defeat at White Hart Lane in the fourth round of the FA Cup in January 1933.

lose the return at Prenton Park on Boxing Day 13-4, which remains the club record defeat. It was the day Tranmere centre-forward 'Bunny' Bell scored nine of the goals, an individual League record. They overcame that setback to finish a respectable seventh, fifteen points adrift of champions Chesterfield – only one team gained promotion from this division.

Walsh enjoyed a great season, scoring a club record: thirty-two League goals and thirty-seven goals in all competitions to finish top scorer in the division, but not all the players fared so well. Remarkably, eight of the fourteen new players left the club during the season. Attendances remained a worry; not one five-figure gate was attracted while there were nine that dipped below 5,000.

Mellor retained only fourteen players for the 1936/37 season as he made eleven signings, with Walsh among those to leave – he headed to Scotland and signed for Hearts. Latics' new-look side found themselves among the pacesetters until early February, when they lost at home to top-of-the table Stockport County. That loss proved the turning point of the campaign and they lost confidence, eventually finishing fourth and nine points behind champions Stockport, who completed a League double over Latics.

Irish international centre-forward Tommy Davis, signed from New Brighton for £250 in June 1935, broke Walsh's club record by scoring thirty-three League goals, which still stands to this day, and thirty-eight in all competitions. There was minimal transfer activity before the 1937/38 campaign due to the continued financial constraints, with only three arrivals.

Davis surprisingly found himself out of the team at the start of the season following the goalscoring exploits of Jack Diamond, who in the final practice game scored a hat-trick for the reserves in the opening half hour, changed sides at half-time and promptly scored another treble for the seniors. Diamond, who had made only one first-team appearance following his signing from Bury the previous March, was elevated into the starting line-up and repaid Mellor by scoring five goals in the first four games. And it was his continued good form (he finished the season as seventeen-goal top scorer) that prompted Latics to allow Davis to join Tranmere in February 1938.

Latics enjoyed another successful season, again finishing fourth, this time only five points behind champions Tranmere. It was a campaign that mirrored 1929/30 as Latics at one stage topped the table before losing their way at the end of the campaign – they suffered three damaging defeats in their last five games when three victories would have seen them crowned champions.

Latics had signed inside-forward Ronald Ferrier from Manchester United for a four-figure fee in March, but he arrived too late to ignite a promotion bid. George Milligan was one of three high-profile departures in the summer of 1938, as he joined Everton in a £3,150 deal. His departure broke up one of the strongest half-back lines in Division Three North. Four of the six summer signings were forwards, though only two of the new front men, Ernest Wright (Chesterfield) and David Halford (Bolton) would make a sizeable impression.

Latics made a great start to the 1938/39 season, gaining five wins and one draw from their first six games, and kept up their good form until December, when four straight defeats effectively ended their promotion challenge and crowds almost halved, causing further financial hardship. The last three League games were all at Boundary Park, with a highest attendance of 3,484. Earlier, the visit of Hartlepool attracted a crowd of just 2,708. Latics eventually finished fifth, eighteen points adrift of champions Barnsley, while Ferrier finished his first full season as top scorer with twenty-four League and Cup goals.

Only three matches of the 1939/40 campaign had been completed when the season was aborted in early September due to the outbreak of the Second World War. Latics were soon back in action, though, in the quickly convened North West Division of the War Regional League, in which they played twenty-two fixtures. They finished fifth in the ten-team competition, with Ferrier banging in nineteen goals in twenty-one appearances and nine others in friendlies.

It was a new-look Latics side, though, as Latics borrowed former favourites Billy Porter, Fred Worrall, Tom Butler, Cliff Chadwick, Arthur Buckley, George Milligan and Billy Walsh, who all returned to help the club. Latics won half their matches, though there was a 11-2 defeat at Blackpool, while the visit of Blackburn Rovers attracted the lowest ever recorded attendance for a first-team game, with only 412 at Boundary Park.

The second season of wartime football saw positions determined on goal average as clubs didn't play the same number of games. Blackpool and Bolton, for example, didn't enter the competition until the second half of the campaign, while Hull City dropped out in April.

The 1941/42 season was split into two competitions pre- and post-Christmas and Latics didn't prosper well in either. A visit of Halifax Town on 6 December attracted a crowd of 479, the second lowest recorded crowd at the ground.

Channel Islander Sylvester Rabey, who made five appearances for Latics at outside right, became the first fatality when he was killed during war training in the summer of 1942. It was another season of struggle for Latics in 1942/43, as they won only nine and drew six of their thirty-eight matches in another campaign played with the same format as the previous year. But it was viewed as an achievement to fulfil all their fixtures due to the war and Latics used a total of forty-three players. Far less importance was attached to results – the priority was keeping football alive in the town.

Latics enjoyed their most successful wartime campaign in 1943/44, enjoying some notable victories against First and Second Division clubs – no mean achievement for a side from the third tier.

Following an indifferent time in 1944/45, Latics' directors decided to advertise for a team manager to give Mellor a break, as he had done the job for almost a decade alongside being club secretary. Latics received over sixty applications, and in February appointed Frank Womack, who had previously managed Torquay, Grimsby, Leicester and Notts County. As a player, he had captained Birmingham for seventeen consecutive seasons.

Latics had sixty players and staff actively involved with the forces and suffered a number of casualties. Beaumont Ratcliffe was wounded and taken prisoner of war, Thomas Jones lost both feet, while Tommy Parnaby was also seriously hurt and Rabey sadly didn't return home. Though the Second World War had ended, football didn't return to normal for 1945/46, as there was another new set up – the Third Division, North West Championship. Latics again toiled on the pitch, finishing bottom.

Latics offered shares to the public in May 1946 to raise £6,000 to pay off liabilities and put the club on a sound financial footing for the new campaign. Womack re-signed outside-right Tommy Butler for £500 from Middlesbrough and brought in others, including Richard Witham (Blackpool), Bill Blackshaw (Manchester City), John Ormandy (Southend) and Fred Howe (Grimsby Town).

Latics' return to Third Division North action was steady, and they reached New Year with a hope they may be able to push up the table in the second part of the campaign, having beaten Halifax Town 6-1 at home on New Year's Day. However, the season would soon unravel as they would win only three further matches from twenty attempts, finishing nineteenth out of twenty-two clubs and just avoiding having to apply for re-election.

Centre-forward Howe, who was almost thirty-four years of age when he signed for Latics, proved an inspired capture, scoring twenty goals in thirty-one appearances during his one season at Boundary Park. Womack, frustrated by the lack of resources, resigned in early April, and in June he was replaced by Billy Wootton, the little known manager of Northwich Victoria. This was a surprise appointment as footballing legends Stan Cullis and Sam Barkas were on the shortlist of three and Wootton had been the rank outsider.

The most significant of Wootton's signings for the 1947/48 season were centre-forward Eric Gemmell from Manchester City and inside-forward Bill Haddington from Bradford City. Gemmell would become Latics' all-time leading scorer. Latics also suffered the misfortune of signing John Divers from Greenock Morton, only for the Scottish international to injure his knee on his debut and never play for the club again. He had been appointed captain and was viewed as a leader.

Wootton had a baptism of fire, failing to win any of his first eight League matches in which Latics picked up only two points and scored a meagre five goals. Latics didn't record their first win until the last Saturday in September, when they won 6-0 at Darlington where Haddington scored his first goals for the club, a splendid hat-trick. The victory sparked shoots of recovery as Latics finished eleventh and well clear of danger. They had also signed centre-forward Lewis Brook from Huddersfield Town in March, and his return of seven goals in eleven appearances helped maintain the momentum.

Bill Blackshaw scored four goals in a 5-1 win at Halifax Town on the last day of the season to take his season's total to seventeen, edging out Haddington for the honour of leading scorer, who would end with fifteen.

There was continued improvement under Wootton as Latics climbed to sixth place at the end of the 1948/49 campaign. This was no mean achievement, bearing in mind Latics made another horrendous start, picking up only one point from their first eight League games. The upturn in fortunes coincided with the introduction of Gemmell into the side in early October. He went on to score twenty-three League and Cup goals and, coupled with twenty-two from Haddington, it was small wonder Latics began to shoot up the table. The season ended with Wootton being rewarded with a new two-year contract.

That season, Latics also made an audacious attempt to sign legend Wilf Mannion, who was in dispute with Middlesbrough and spent time training with Latics. Shareholders and supporters were asked to help raise part of the £25,000 asking price as the 'Mannion Fund' was launched. Mannion, one of British football's all-time greats, was keen to join Latics and one of the club's directors found him a job in the town, but his dispute with 'Boro was settled and the transfer never happened.

Latics turned down sizeable bids for three of their prized assets, and they went into the 1949/50 campaign full of optimism in what was viewed as one of the most open seasons for some time. However, it was a season blighted by inconsistency as Latics finished a disappointing eleventh, though there was a modicum of success in the FA Cup as they reached the third round where there was a lucrative tie against Newcastle United.

Latics had no answer to the Jackie Milburn-inspired Magpies, who triumphed 7-2 at Boundary Park, though the blow was cushioned by an attendance of 31,706. Haddington eclipsed Gemmell for the top goalscoring honour, with twenty-four in the League and Cup.

The club sold Channel Islander Bill Spurdle to Manchester City for a club record £10,000 in January 1950. He would become the first Channel Islander to play in the final of the FA Cup in 1955. However, his departure was offset by the signings of Bill Ormond (Blackpool) and Bobby McIlvenny (Merthyr Tydfil), who cost £3,000. Both would become favourites at Boundary Park.

There was a failed bid by the Shareholders' Association to oust three retiring directors as there unrest off the field.

Latics made yet another awful start to a season in 1950/51 – they had become a feature of Wootton's reign – after they won only one of their first eight matches. It resulted in Wootton resigning in late September.

ENGLAND LEGEND APPOINTED PLAYER-MANAGER

November was an eventful month as Latics sold crowd favourite Haddington to Manchester City for £8,000, but then splashed out a club record £15,000 to appoint Middlesbrough and former England captain George Hardwick as their player-manager. There was a crowd of 21,742 at Boundary Park for Hardwick's debut, a goalless draw against Lincoln City. The directors' bold decision to appoint Hardwick was vindicated as Latics made a fine recovery to finish fifteenth and well clear of danger, aided by the twenty-two League and Cup goals scored by Gemmell. There was also a run to the third round of the FA Cup, where Latics lost 4-1 at Manchester United in front of a 37,161 crowd.

Despite a large bank overdraft, Hardwick managed to sign four experienced players, notably Peter McKennan, a thirty-three-year-old inside-forward from his former club, Middlesbrough, and they went into the manager's first full campaign full of hope. Latics certainly hit the ground running at the start of the 1951/52 season after a strenuous build-up; they won six and drew the three remaining games from their first nine fixtures.

 It continued to be a much-improved campaign as Latics finished fourth, twelve points behind champions Lincoln. It would definitely have been far less of a deficit had Latics not been hit by injuries to a number of key players.

The undoubted high came in mid-January, when Latics beat Chester 11-2 at snowbound Boundary Park, where Gemmell set the club's individual scoring record with seven – his first six in succession. The entertainment value could not be faulted as Latics scored a total of ninety-four League and Cup goals, Gemmell leading the way with twenty-nine and McKennan contributing nineteen.

That season, goalkeeper Eddie Hopkinson became the youngest player to appear for the club, aged sixteen years and seventy-five days. He made three appearances as an amateur, including the 11-2 win against Chester. Hopkinson was due that summer to sign as a professional, but an administrative blunder meant he was not notified and, believing he was unwanted, he signed for Bolton Wanderers for whom he still holds the record of 519 League appearances between 1956–70. He was also capped by England, to compound the agony for Latics.

Hardwick signed Tommy Lowrie, a tough Glaswegian wing-half from Aberdeen, on the eve of the 1952/53 season, and he was viewed as the final piece of the jigsaw. The manager's confidence that this would be Latics' year was reinforced by another excellent start as they were unbeaten for the opening thirteen games, and by January they were well established at the top of the table.

PLAYER-MANAGER: George Hardwick, the former Middlesbrough and England full-back, leads out Latics at Boundary Park.

TRAINING: Player-manager George Hardwick (*far right*) makes a point in training.

OLD TRAFFORD:
Action from Latics'
FA Cup tie against
Manchester United
in January 1951.

Then the cracks began to appear as Latics, hit by injuries and players losing form, managed only one win in an eleven-game spell between mid-January and the end of March.

Latics regained their form to end the season unbeaten in their final nine League matches as they pipped Port Vale for top spot by only one point. After forty-six years of League football, Latics had won their first championship, and they also became the first club from Lancashire to win promotion from Third Division North to Division Two. Gemmell's goals were again pivotal as he scored twenty-five in League and Cup games, while Ormond and McKennan finished with twelve apiece.

Hardwick set his goal as consolidation as Latics began their 1953/54 campaign, believing his side would finish with a comfortable top-half spot in the Second Division. How wrong Hardwick was. Latics endured a tortuous campaign in which they finished bottom, cut adrift by a six-point margin. They kicked off with a thrilling 4-4 draw at Luton Town, but had to wait nine matches before recording their first victory, a 1-0 home success against Lincoln.

Latics found themselves anchored at the foot of the table for most of the season and they managed to amass only eight victories and twenty-five points as Hardwick lacked the finances to equip the side for life in a higher division.

The acute shortage of goals was underlined by McIlvenny finishing top scorer with six League goals and a further two in the Cup. Club record goalscorer Gemmell had been transferred to Crewe in February, to the angst of fans.

Latics also broke new ground in 1953/54, when hospital radio broadcast commentaries from Boundary Park. One of them was the last match of the season, when Everton won 4-0 to clinch promotion – a sizeable majority of the 30,072 crowd had travelled from Merseyside. McIlvenny was transferred to Bury for £2,000 after Latics refused him a guaranteed maximum benefit of £750, but on the eve of the new season, centre-forward Don Travis returned from Chester in a £570 deal.

CHAMPIONS: The Third Division (North) title-winning team of 1952/53, the first championship ever won by Latics.

HOT SHOT: Eric Gemmell, who held Latics' all-time scoring record until it was beaten by Roger Palmer, scores the first goal of a hat-trick in a 4-1 win against Lincoln City in 1951.

There was a relegation hangover as Latics won only one of their first eight League games, and average attendances tumbled by 10,000, adding to the financial pressures – Hardwick didn't spend one penny in the transfer market during the season.

Latics failed to score in seven of their first fifteen games, finding themselves languishing in eighteenth place. They arrested the slide, embarking upon a successful run in the winter months in which they climbed to seventh before slipping back to tenth by the season's end.

Hardwick was forced to develop young players, with insider-forward Kenny Chaytor handed a debut at sixteen years and eleven months. He went on to make eighteen League appearances, scoring eight goals, including a hat-trick against Mansfield.

Travis, who had failed to impress in his first spell at the club, certainly confounded his critics on his return by scoring thirty-two League goals in his first season back at Boundary Park – he came within one of equally Davis' club record of League goals in one season.

The 1955/56 season was one to forget as Latics finished twentieth in Division Three North with only four teams beneath them in the table. Hardwick had had enough and resigned at the end of the campaign. Latics managed only one win in their first eleven League matches and that set the tone for the campaign as a whole. Between Christmas Eve and 3 March, for example, they went twelve League games without a win. Latics ended the dismal run with a 6-1 home win against Barrow, This sparked an improved run and they won three and drew five of their final ten games to remain clear of the bottom clubs.

Former Latics' player Ted Goodier, who appeared for them in their Second Division days between 1925–31, was appointed as Hardwick's successor. He had previously had a successful spell as manager of Rochdale and stint at Wigan Athletic. Despite a major overhaul of the squad – nineteen players were signed at a total cost of £1,125 and seven left during the season – Goodier failed to improve fortunes. Latics had another miserable campaign in which they finished nineteenth, winning only two of their last twenty-eight fixtures, which negated a half decent opening to the season, in which they were in seventh place in November.

There were also reports of dressing room unrest. It soon became clear that there were problems and it was a far from united camp as four players asked to leave, prompting a worrying slide down the table. Travis, who finished top scorer for the third successive season with fourteen goals, was one of the unhappy players. He left for Yeovil in the summer of 1957. Inside-forward David Pearson, who had scored twelve goals, was also surprisingly sold to Rochdale in March.

Goodier had another major clearout as he kicked off 1957/58 with virtually a new team taking to the field. Spurdle returned to Boundary Park after spells at Manchester City and Port Vale, and among the other new arrivals was the distinguished Eddie Shimwell from Blackpool.

It was also an important season for Latics as Division Three North and South were to merge from 1958/59. The bottom twelve clubs from each division would form the Division Four, so Latics needed a high finish to avoid finding themselves in the basement. When they began 1958 with a run of ten games without a win, they looked destined for a bottom half finish. They almost avoided it after improved fortunes in March and April, and they went into the last game of the season at Darlington knowing a win would secure a top half finish. Latics lost 3-1 and were left one point and two positions away from securing a place in Division Three.

Centre-forward Gerry Duffy, who had been recruited from non-League Middlewich, for whom he scored over a century of goals, was top scorer with seventeen in League and Cup, followed closely by inside-forward Peter Neale with sixteen.

Goodier resigned in June 1958, and the next month Norman Dodgin was, who, aged thirty-seven, was one of the youngest managers in football. Dodgin was only thirty-one when he embarked upon his managerial career at Exeter, and he also served at Yeovil and Barrow before arriving at Boundary Park. He had gained a reputation for developing young players, something that appealed due to Latics' lack of cash.

The Football League's experiment of four up, four down gave Latics renewed hope of a speedy return to Division Three. However, this quickly disappeared as it turned out to be the worst season in the club's history. They finished in the bottom four, which meant having to apply for re-election from their peers at the League's annual meeting.

Latics managed to win only two of their first nine games, and continued to lose games at an alarming rate, especially between mid-January and mid-March, when they lost nine out of ten games and drew the other as they found themselves doomed. Strangely, they finished well with six wins and a draw from their last ten games, but it proved too little, too late.

Latics retained their League status and Dodgin was provided with leeway to strengthen his squad. There were seven signings in readiness for the 1959/60 season, but it proved another one to forget, both on and off the field. There had been early promise as Latics beat Reading and Crystal Palace in their opening two games, but that quickly disappeared as they then went sixteen games without a win, a sequence that included twelve defeats. Indeed, Latics managed only eight victories in their forty-six League games, accumulating only twenty-eight points as they finished second bottom of the basement division and only one point clear of bottom club Hartlepool United.

Latics had to seek re-election for the second successive season. They scored forty-one goals, which was fewer than any other team in the division, and conceded eighty-three. Then, as if things couldn't get any worse, came match-fixing allegations in the local press. This involved Latics' players, five of whom were interviewed by Oldham Police, who sent a file to the Director of Public Prosecutions, but it was decided there would be no further police action.

Dodgin's contract was cancelled by mutual agreement following two disastrous seasons. The club was undoubtedly at its lowest ebb, with chairman Gordon Bloor again warning the club was on the brink of folding, declaring the financial outlook was bleak. Mr Bloor suggested Latics' directors would resign en bloc if suitable investors could be found and were able to improve the club's fortunes.

In the wake of this depressing backdrop, the only ray of sunshine was that Latics were re-elected to huge sighs of relief. Gatehead, who finished one place above them, were voted out and replaced by Peterborough. Two days before the club sought re-election, Danny McLennan was confirmed as Dodgin's successor as Latics had been impressed by the job he had done at Berwick Rangers, where he cleared a five-figure debt at the Scottish club and lifted the team into the top six of the Scottish Second Division.

FRIZZELL BECOMES KEY SIGNING

McLennan spoke of his delight that the week before he signed he was delighted to learn that Latics had bought Jimmy Frizzell from Greenock Morton for £1,500, a player and later manager who would play a pivotal role in transforming the fortunes of the club. There was further drama as McLennan's stay lasted only one month, as he sensationally quit after accepting a better offer from Stirling Albion.

Secretary Frank Buckley took over as acting manager until the appointment of Manchester United legend Jack Rowley on 2 August, only eighteen days before the 1960/61 season kicked off, which was hardly ideal for preparation.

Rowley made an inauspicious start as Latics lost their first four matches, and a first win wasn't registered until the seventh attempt as another season of struggle and strife looked likely. The new manager eventually began to stamp his own mark on the team and the season lifted off in October, the month Rowley signed centre-forward Bert Lister and full-back Ken Branagan for a joint fee of £10,000 from Manchester City, from whom he also bought legendary inside-forward Bobby Johnstone a fortnight later for £4,000. He also signed outside-left Bob Rackley on a free from Bristol Rovers.

When former Scotland international Johnstone, who earlier had become the first player to score in successive FA Cup finals while playing for Manchester City and was regarded as one of the great inside-forwards of post-war football, signed for Latics, it gave the club an enormous lift following several seasons in the doldrums. There was a crowd of 17,116, the highest at Boundary Park for six-and-a-half years, for Johnstone's debut, a 5-2 victory against Exeter City in which the thirty-one-year-old scored.

The new arrivals helped spark a rebirth of the town's footballing hopes in a season that could easily have witnessed the end of professional football in Oldham. Latics, who had successfully been re-elected for each of the previous two seasons, had no such worries as Rowley lifted them to a comfortable mid-table twelfth place, the highlight of the season being a run of eight straight victories between December and February.

Lister immediately made his mark, scoring twenty-one League and Cup goals in only twenty-seven appearances, while Johnstone contributed thirteen goals, and Frizzell, an inside-forward in his early days at Latics, scored ten.

Latics went into the 1961/62 season believing they could challenge for promotion after Rowley signed nine new players, the notable capture being Stirling Albion winger John Colquhoun for £4,000, and Bristol City centre-half Alan Williams, who cost £1,000. Johnstone also re-signed after initially rejecting new terms, and positive vibes were emerging from Boundary Park.

Right: LEGEND: Former
Scottish international Bobby
Johnstone signs for Latics from
Hibernian for £4,000 in 1960,
watched by manager
Jack Rowley.

Below: JINKING JOHNSTONE:
Bobby Johnstone leaves an
opponent for dead in one of his
first matches for Latics.

While a bid for promotion failed to materialise (they finished a disappointing eleventh), it was still viewed as the finest season for many years. Latics reached the fourth round of the FA Cup where they played Liverpool at Boundary Park, and were unlucky to lose 2-1 in front of a crowd of 41,733. It was the season when Bill Shankly's Liverpool were crowned Second Division champions.

Frizzell had a season to remember, scoring twenty-five goals in all competitions, while Lister hit twenty-one and Johnstone twelve. It was also the season when floodlights first appeared at Boundary Park, and they were switched on for the first time on a Tuesday night in October, when Burnley were the visitors for a friendly. The following month there was a friendly under the lights against Yugoslavian side OFK Belgrade.

The motto around Boundary Park for 1962/63 was promotion or bust, but the words of chairman Frank Armitage became almost too prophetic. A failure to win promotion would have been catastrophic as the team had cost £45,000 to assemble, making it the most expensive in the club's history. Summer signings Bob Ledger, who cost £5,750 from Huddersfield Town, Jim Bowie, Peter McCall and Bill Marshall all made a significant contribution as Rowley's third season ended in triumph.

UP FOR THE CUP: Fans among the 41,733 crowd at Boundary Park for the FA Cup fourth-round tie against Liverpool in January 1962.

Latics hit the ground running, and it was not until the first week of October that they tasted their first defeat. Indeed, they suffered only three losses until late February, when the wheels fell off in a spectacular way. There were some magical moments, none more so than the never-to-be-forgotten club record 11-0 win against Southport on Boxing Day, when Lister scored six to eclipse winger Colin Whitaker, who had scored a first-half hat-trick.

After heading the table for most of the campaign, Latics suffered an almighty wobble when they failed to win in six matches as the strain started to tell. Luckily, they regained their poise, composure and form in time to finish second behind Brentford, who were crowned champions.

Latics finished the season in style, defeating Hartlepool United 6-1 to secure the runners-up spot on goal difference from Crewe Alexandra. The six goals took their total to ninety-five League goals, with Lister scoring thirty-two of them, as well as a further three in the League Cup. Whitaker, signed in the October of that season, weighed in with eighteen, and Colquhoun fourteen. The celebrations were cut short, however, as three days after the last match Rowley was dismissed following a split in the boardroom, with a number of directors allegedly wanting to pick the team.

There were over thirty applicants, including one from former manager Hardwick, to succeed Rowley. Les McDowall was appointed in June 1963, one month after he lost his job after thirteen years in charge of Manchester City. He had won promotion from Division Two and then guided the team to FA Cup finals in 1955 and '56, but resigned following their relegation.

McDowell admitted he was lucky to take over with the club riding on the crest of a wave, and Latics more than held their own in Division Three, finishing a highly respectable ninth. His mantra was that if it wasn't broken, why fix it. He went to maintain the continuity and stability that had earned promotion.

Latics had no difficulty adjusting to life in a higher division as they won eight of their first eleven League fixtures to find themselves top of the table in early October. By January they were still second. Any hope of promotion then disappeared as Latics suffered six defeats and one draw from their next seven fixtures. The signing of Scottish inside- forward Bobby Craig from St Johnstone for £5,000 in March helped arrest the slide in what was a disappointing second half to the season.

There was a quiet optimism that Latics would be able to build on their previous season's satisfactory debut season in Division Three and challenge for promotion in 1964/65. However, the campaign could not have turned out more differently as it developed into a desperate bid to avoid relegation. An opening day 5-1 home defeat by Grimsby Town set the tone as Latics won only two of their first seventeen League matches, which left them rooted at the bottom of the table.

This called for reinforcements and McDowell splashed the cash, paying £10,000 to Blackpool for Barrie Martin, who became the club's second costliest signing. He also brought in one-time Manchester United golden boy Albert Quixall for £8,500, and Bury winger Tony Bartley for £7,500, while Lister left to join Rochdale.

There was a mini revival midseason, when Latics won seven out of nine League games, but other than that it was a season to forget as they finished twentieth and only avoided relegation by one place. The resulting fall in attendances (the average was 8,000 as opposed

OLDHAM EVENING CHRONICLE, Thursday December 27th 1962

Goal No. 1—Colin Whitaker blasts home a right-footer.

There's another one! Southport's keeper looks back bewildered, as Lister hits No. 7.

Goal No. 3—and the first of Lister's half dozen, as he hooks the ball past Harris.

Colquhoun joins in the revels as he cracks home goal No. 4.

Whitaker completes his hat-trick with a spectacular cross-shot.

And now Ledger (left) gets in the act with a flashing drive.

8...9...10—it's 11-goal Latics in record win

OLDHAM ATHLETIC 11, SOUTHPORT 0

THE ardent rugby supporter summed it up in a sentence . . . . "But somebody told me this team had no punch in front of goal!" Yes, Athletic really confounded their critics with their Boxing Day bonanza. Producing a goal avalanche to match the Arctic weather conditions at Boundary Park they wrote themselves a new page in the soccer record books.

With the tousle-haired, double-hat-trick-man, Bert Lister, leading the goal riot, they laid on a Christmas feast to end all feasts.

For 15,000 fans this fantastic football fiesta left even the turkey and stuffing in the shade. Poor Southport never knew what hit them.

I suppose you could say it had to happen sometime. Athletic, with nothing better than a three-goal win to their credit so far this term, just had to hit the golden goal trail sooner or later.

But not even the most fanatical fan could have expected this 11-goal

BIGGEST WIN

Athletic's win was a record for the Fourth Division and the club's biggest-ever win, beating the 11—2 defeat of Chester ten years ago. It was Southport's biggest defeat.

soccer spectacle. Not only were Athletic in blistering goal form, they were brilliant in every department.

Under conditions which at best could only be described as atrocious, Athletic skated over the snow to the proudest moment in the club's history.

Yet even this glorious win brought its disappointments. Firstly, with a seven-goal lead at half-time, Athletic went all out to create a new club record.

One short

They did their utmost to better the 11-goal tally notched against Chester back in 1952—and no one tried harder than hero Lister, who hit four of his six goals in that final 45-minute period.

In the closing minutes, Athletic raged even fiercer than the driving snowstorm, which threatened to wipe out the game. But they couldn't make the dozen.

Disappointment No. 2 was for schemer-in-chief Bobby Johnstone. While he watched his fellow forwards take large helpings of the goal feast Bobby just couldn't get his name on the scoresheet.

One block-buster of a goal

disallowed and two great saves from goal-keeper Joe Harris almost added up to a conspiracy to cheat Athletic's top - class architect.

But if Bobby didn't get among the goals he had his share of the glory. Like an impudent snowman, he was all over the snow-covered pitch, prodding and probing, reducing the shattered Southport defence to a state of total collapse.

This wasn't one man's day, however. Not even Lister, with his superb six-goal haul, could claim that.

Narrow angle

There were the brilliant efforts of flying-winger Colin Whitaker. He started the fun with a first-half hat-trick that soon had the icicles melting on the terraces.

There was the non-stop display from his inside partner, Johnny Colquhoun. What a great first-half this terrier-like little Scot had!

There was an equally great first-half display by Bob Ledger crowned with a gem of a goal, which he crashed home at an angle through the narrowest of gaps between goal-keeper and post.

And then, of course, there was the performance of the defence, a complete unit, which never gave the Southport attack so much as the hint of a chance, a unit which provided a solid springboard for the incessant Athletic attacks.

While we are mentioning the glories, spare a thought for Southport 'keeper Joe Harris. Eleven back-breaking, heart-rending times he picked that ball out of the back of his net, yet, on the whole, he played a fine game. He pulled off a number of remarkable saves to keep the rampaging Athletic attack at bay.

Packed with punch

At the same time, spare a thought for Athletic 'keeper Johnny Bollands. Often a lone figure in the Athletic half, he came near to double pneumonia in his role as Athletic's coldest spectator.

Yes, this was a rip-roaring team

triumph—a scintillating success, which sent the sub-normal temperatures soaring.

So outclassed were Southport that at times it seemed they were playing the game on roller skates. Athletic's soccer artistry, packed with pep and punch, left them skidding all over the place.

Just for the record, and for the benefit of those doubting fans who claimed that Southport must have been playing in studless boots, the members were wearing regulation boots, studded equally as well as Athletic's.

Only left-winger Bill Perry decided on a second-half change of studs but it didn't make any difference—he didn't see anything of the ball.

No, it was Athletic's fire and determination which led them to this unequalled triumph. The efforts of players like Lister, Colquhoun and Williams, who did not acknowledge any danger in playing on such a treacherous surface.

A final coincidence note: Referee J. Mitchell, of Prescot, told apprehensive Athletic officials before the game, "I never see home teams win. Of the last eight games I have refereed, five have been away wins and the other three draw."

ATHLETIC: Bollands; Branagan, Marshall; McCall, Williams, Scott; Ledger, Johnstone, Lister, Colquhoun, Whitaker.

SOUTHPORT: Harris; Payne, Griffiths; Peat, Durrell, Rutherford; Boues, Fielding, Bhoe, Cooper, Perry.

Referee: Mr. J. Mitchell (Prescot).

Attendance: 15,000.

DIVISION FOUR

	P	W	D	L	F	A	Pts
ATHLETIC							
Brentford							
Mansfield T.							
Gillingham							
Crewe Alex.							
ROCHDALE							
Torquay							
Workington							
Aldershot							
Darlington							
Oxford Utd.							
Barrow							
Newport Co.							
Lincoln City							
Chesterfield							
Stockport Co.							
Doncaster Rov.							
Tranmere Rov.							
Chester							
Southport							
Bradford P.A.							
Exeter City							
York City							
Hartlepool U.							

CHRISTMAS CHEER: How the Oldham Evening Chronicle reported on the record-breaking 11-0 home win against Southport on Boxing Day 1962.

SIX-HITTER: Bert Lister scores one of his six goals in the record-breaking 11-0 win against Southport.

BIG FREEZE: Snow clearing at Boundary Park during the winter of 1962/63, which was one of the worst on record.

PROMOTION:
The team that finished runners-up in Division Four in 1962/63.

to 14,000 during the promotion campaign two seasons earlier) brought about a new cash crisis and worries about the club surviving.

McDowall, who lost his job at Easter, was replaced in the summer by Gordon Hurst, who had played for Latics as an amateur during the Second World War. He later enjoyed a distinguished career with Charlton Athletic, appearing for them in the final of the FA Cup in 1947. Later, he returned to Oldham to work for the council and became part-time manager of Latics' reserves.

Hurst, who lost players of the calibre of Johnstone, Williams, McCall and Martin, was unable to arrest the slide as Latics managed a meagre three wins from the opening twenty-two League matches of the 1965/66 campaign to find themselves bottom of the table.

Wealthy Cheshire businessman Ken Bates had in December become chairman and financial saviour following five weeks of secret negotiations. Suddenly, there was a new buzz about the club as Mr Bates splashed out a club record £20,000 for Burnley's Ian Towers, along with £8,000 for Blackburn's Reg Blore and £7,500 for Frank Large from Carlisle. Half-back Dennis Stevens also arrived from Everton and full-back Bill Asprey from Stoke. This was reflected by the crowd at Boundary Park shooting up to 14,099 for the debuts of Towers, Stevens, Blore and Large, whereas the average home gate up to that point was 6,145.

Latics were paired with the then mighty West Ham – their side contained Bobby Moore, Geoff Hurst and Martin Peter, who would become World Cup winners six months later – in the third round of the FA Cup. Latics drew 2-2 at Boundary Park in front of a crowd of 25,035 and would probably have won had Quixall not missed a penalty. They lost the replay 2-1 with 35,330 at Upton Park.

Hurst's reign soon came to an end as he was replaced by Jimmy McIlroy, the Burnley legend and Northern Ireland international signing a five-year contract, with Hurst remaining as his assistant. Despite an outlay of almost £50,000 in the transfer market, new-look Latics managed only nine wins in their final twenty-seven League matches to again finish twentieth, and they once more avoided relegation by just one place.

Mr Bates again provided financial backing for McIlroy to sign Keith Bebbington and George Kinnell from Stoke City for a joint fee of £25,000, and Bournemouth goalkeeper David Best for an outlay of £15,000. He also funded a revamp of Boundary Park, which included the installation of private hospitality boxes. Latics are believed to be the first club to have them, so he was clearly a visionary back in the mid-sixties.

Latics made an encouraging start, winning five of their first seven games, with Kinnell an instant hit as he scored eight goals in twelve appearances before being sold to Sunderland for a club record £20,000 only three months after his arrival. It was an unpopular move, though the fans were somewhat appeased by the £12,000 capture of Wolves midfielder Ken Knighton, though by this time Latics were on the slide. Large also departed in December to Northampton Town in a £14,000 deal. Latics won only once in six League games in December, and from January only a further seven victories were secured as they finished tenth.

There was FA Cup joy as Latics reached the third round when they played Wolves in front of a 24,968 crowd at Boundary Park, where they drew 2-2 having held a two-goal lead until the dying stages. They lost the replay 4-1.

McIlroy boldly turned to youth later in the season, introducing Ian Wood, Ronnie Blair and Les Chapman, three players who would later become Latics legends. Towers enjoyed a rich vein of form, scoring twenty-seven League goals as he finished top scorer for a second successive season, the previous one having only signed for the club mid-term.

Latics were groundbreakers in the summer of 1967 as they embarked upon a preseason tour of Rhodesia and Malawi, a huge adventure in those long-gone days. They played eleven matches, winning ten and suffering just one loss. It was a controversial tour due to the political regime in Rhodesia, with the matter raised in the House of Commons, but it was described as an overwhelming success.

Later, McIlroy took Latics to Northern Ireland for a second successive summer and, in total, Latics played a staggering nineteen preseason matches, though they lost only one of them.

Perhaps that exhaustive schedule had a bearing as Latics made a dreadful start to the 1967/68 season. They won only one of their first twelve matches and picked up a meagre four points, finding themselves bottom of the table. Then, without a major overhaul, Latics suddenly hit a rich vein of form, recording seven straight victories which, incredibly, only saw them climb five places up the table.

McIroy, who had signed Irish forward Eric Magee from Glenavon for £4,000 preseason, later added Alan Philpott, a £7,500 capture from Stoke, and Blackburn Rovers' Walter Joyce. Mid-December saw a further overhaul as Knighton was sold to Preston for a club record £35,000 and Ledger to Mansfield for £3,000, the latter's place at centre-forward taken by Laurie Sheffield, a £17,000 buy from Rotherham.

Latics clearly missed the drive of Knighton and goals of Ledger (he had hit eleven in sixteen League games before his move and would still finish as that season's leading scorer) as they lost five in a row and didn't register a win in seven League games. They eventually arrested the slide to collect seventeen points in the final two months of the season to finish sixteenth.

There was turmoil on and off the pitch before the start of the 1968/69 season with no major signings, Towers leaving for Bury and McIlroy reported to be considering his future. In addition, there was unrest in the boardroom. After a terrible start to the season, in which Latics conceded eleven goals in their first three League games, McIlroy tendered his resignation and directors Harry Massey, Ronnie Clayton and Arthur Hudson took charge of the team until Rowley returned in late September for a second spell as manager. By that time, Mr Bates had returned from holiday to resign as chairman but remain a director, saying he needed to concentrate on his job rather than football, which he described as an 'expensive hobby.'

Within six months, though, Mr Bates had also resigned as a director and left altogether, and it was against this depressing backdrop that Latics were relegated, finishing in last place as Rowley was unable to revive fortunes. In fairness, Latics, who managed only two wins in the opening four months of the season, did improve massively in the second half of the season, aided by the signings of Southport striker Derek Spence, who scored twelve goals in twenty-three appearances, and the return of Colquhoun following a spell at Scunthorpe. The damage, however, had been inflicted earlier in the campaign as they collected only nine points from twenty-one League matches before Christmas.

Frizzell was also appointed first-team coach, though he continued playing, but his playing appearances weren't as frequent as they once were. If Latics thought they would make an immediate return to Division Three in 1969/70, they were mistaken. The harsh reality of their financial ills saw them finish sixth bottom and at one stage it looked as though they might have to apply for re-election for a third time in the club's history.

Latics were unable to reject decent offers for players and Allan Hunter was transferred to Blackburn for £30,000, followed by Les Chapman to Huddersfield in exchange for David Shaw, plus £35,000. Rowley persuaded England World Cup winner Ray Wilson, one of

MANAGEMENT TEAM: Bobby Collins (*left*), Jimmy Frizzell (*centre*) and Walter Joyce brought success to Latics in the early 1970s.

the best post-war full-backs, to sign after he left Everton, while other arrivals included left-back Maurice Whittle and striker Jim Beardall, both from Blackburn Rovers.

Latics endured a terrible start, winning only four of their first twenty-four matches, and also being knocked out of the FA Cup by non-League South Shields. They were dire times and Rowley paid the price as he was sacked on 29 December.

Frizzell was appointed caretaker manager and fortunes steadily improved, especially after the £8,000 signing of Blackburn striker Jim Fryatt, which proved a huge turning point. Fryatt scored eleven goals in sixteen appearances, while Shaw struck twelve in his debut campaign as Latics clawed their way to safety, finishing sixth bottom.

Frizzell was rewarded with a two-year managerial contract while off the field there was much-needed stability after local businessman John Lowe joined the board and secured the club's future by reaching an agreement with former chairman Mr Bates over repayment of money owed to him. Mr Lowe admitted Mr Bates had the power to close the club, which had been under threat in all directions, as they had also faced re-election and being voted out of the League.

The 1970/71 season provided the dawn of a new era as Latics finally banished years of failure and frustration. After the near disaster of the previous campaign, Frizzell amazingly led Latics to promotion in his first full season as manager, while there was also an added £70,000 cash windfall as Latics won the Ford Sporting League. Teams from all four divisions earned points for scoring goals and had them deducted when players were booked or sent off. Latics won the cash prize each month and an end-of-season bonus with the money used to build the new Broadway Stand, which became known as the Ford Stand.

The two most significant signings made by Frizzell were Bill Cranston, a wing-half bought for £6,000 from Preston where he had been that season's player of the year, and winger Don Heath. Cranston was made captain, and he was an excellent defender and leader on the pitch, while Heath, who helped Swindon win the League Cup the previous year, provided the service for strikers Fryatt and Shaw, who finished with twenty-six and twenty-four goals respectively.

Latics made an encouraging start, and a run of nine wins in ten games between the end of October and start of January catapulted them into second place and genuine promotion candidates. It looked as though Latics might slip up as they went six games without a win in March and, with four matches of the season, they were left clinging on to the fourth and final promotion place, with Chester and Colchester breathing down their necks.

Nerves were eased with a fabulous 4-0 home win against Colchester and 1-0 victory at York City, who would also be promoted. They then made sure of a top-four spot after draws against Workington and Stockport in their last two games. The one slight disappointment was the average attendance of 9,575, bearing in mind it was a promotion-winning campaign in which they had been the division's second leading scorers with eighty-eight League goals.

The 1971/72 season was one of consolidation as newly promoted Latics more than held their own in Division Three, finishing eleventh. It was also a season of transition as Fryatt and Tommy Bryceland moved on to Southend and St Mirren respectively after being unable to set the higher division alight.

WINNINGS: The new Broadway Stand takes shape. It was built with the proceeds from winning the Ford Sporting League in 1970/71.

GOING UP: The team that won promotion from Division Four in 1970/71.

Frizzell pulled off another master stroke by getting Blackburn centre-half Dick Mulvaney on a free transfer after he had been initially listed at £50,000. Latics failed to repeat the previous season's goalscoring exploits as Shaw, who found the net nineteen times, lacked decent support. However, significantly, it was a season when young players like Ian Robins and Keith Hicks, two future stalwarts, would break into the team.

Latics maintained the improvement in 1972/73, as they finished fourth in Division Three. Indeed, but for a disappointing finish to the season they would surely have won promotion as they were only three points shy of a top-two place. They had topped the table in January, but failed to win in February and slipped to seventh spot.

After starting March with back-to-back victories, Latics won only three of their last twelve League games, which coincided with the club record £80,000 sale of striker Shaw to West Brom, the goals drying up after his departure. He had scored eighteen goals in all competitions up to that point, while Ian Wood was an ever-present for the third time in four seasons.

Bobby Collins became the oldest player to appear for the club. The former Celtic, Leeds and Scotland legend had been appointed player-coach in October, and his ninth and final playing appearance came at forty-two years and sixty-three days in a goalless draw at home to Rochdale on Good Friday.

There was to be no slip up in 1973/74 as Latics won the Division Three title. It was only the second championship the club had won since becoming a League club in 1907. The team displayed a steely determination to succeed, though there was a stuttering start and faltering finish to the season.

When Latics lost 1-0 at Port Vale on New Year's Day, they found themselves in tenth place and a seemingly irretrievable thirteen points behind leaders Bristol Rovers. They then put together a brilliant run of ten straight victories to ignite a promotion challenge. Three victories in four days over Easter, which included a 2-1 victory at title rivals Bristol Rovers, effectively won them the League.

They tried their hardest to blow promotion for a second successive season as they failed to win in their last four League games, but they finished top by a single point ahead of both runners-up Bristol Rovers and York City, who missed out in third place.

Frizzell also made a key signing in February, buying Bournemouth's stylish winger Alan Groves for a bargain £10,000. But perhaps the most astute capture had been made on the eve of the new season, when Latics paid Aston Villa £15,000 for veteran striker Andy Lochhead. Appointing him as team captain was another inspired move.

Striker Colin Garwood's third season at Boundary Park proved his most productive one as he finished top scorer with seventeen League and Cup goals, while average home attendances showed a marked improvement, rising to 10,356. Latics also created a piece of history that season when their FA Cup third-round tie at Cambridge United became the first-ever Sunday game in professional football, brought about by the industrial unrest that included power blackouts.

Vice-chairman Arthur Hudson summed up the achievement, declaring,

Four years ago when we were bottom of the Fourth Division, we were a joke and commonly referred to as Oldham pathetic. Now we can meet our public with heads held high. We have won back our pride and self respect and are Oldham Athletic again.

CIVIC RECEPTION: Winning the Third Division title in 1973/74 was recognised by Oldham Council.

After two promotions in three years, Latics knew that consolidation was the name of the game in 1974/75 as they returned to the second tier of English football for the first time in twenty years.

They made a decent start, winning four and drawing two of their first eight matches before the harsh realities of the step up began to hit and it became apparent they would be involved in a scrap for survival. Latics failed to win between mid-October and 28 December, a sequence of eleven matches that ended when Manchester United were beaten 1-0 at Boundary Park in a game that will also be remembered for the goal that never was. The photograph of the incident is still displayed at Boundary Park, with Reds' 'keeper Alex Stepney looking on as the ball rebounded back into play after hitting the stanchion in the back of the net and the referee signals to play on.

Latics finished three points clear of the relegation places in eighteenth spot, and their survival would probably not have been achieved but for an inspired midseason transfer deal which saw Les Chapman return and David Holt signed, both in player-exchange deals. Garwood went to Huddersfield Town, with Latics receiving Chapman and £15,000, while Tony Bailey formed part of the deal that brought Holt from Bury, with Latics also splashing out £25,000.

Latics struggled for goals, managing only forty in forty-two League games. Robins finished as the leading marksman with nine, while average home attendances showed a healthy increase to 13,245, but were still below the break-even figure of 15,000.

Quoted by bookmakers at 66/1 for promotion in 1975/76, Latics were joint favourites to be relegated. That was probably influenced by the financial squeeze as Frizzell was unable to strengthen his squad, though Shaw returned from West Brom on a free transfer in October.

Latics, who appointed comedian Eric Sykes to their board of directors, started surprisingly well, and by January found themselves in the giddy heights of fifth place. However, they picked up only eight points from their final sixteen League games to slide to sixth bottom.

CELEBRATIONS: Fans invade the pitch after promotion was secured to the Second Division in 1974.

The threat of relegation loomed in the final month of the season, though they had a five-point safety cushion as they finished seventeenth.

Shaw marked his return by finishing as thirteen-goal top scorer, while in January Wood broke the club's all-time League appearance record when he played his 370th match at Southampton.

Such were the financial restraints that winger George McVitie was sold to Carlisle and striker George Jones left to join Halifax without either being replaced. There were problems with wages, and at the end of the season it was reported the club had a major pay revolt on its hands. These were challenging times for Frizzell, who by the start of the 1976/77 campaign was the longest-serving manager in Division Two. He had been in charge for over seven and a half years.

Frizzell brought in experience in the form of central defender John Hurst on a free transfer from Everton, where he had been a member of their 1969/70 championship side, and striker Vic Halom, a £25,000 capture from Sunderland, for whom he was an FA Cup winner in 1973.

It was a season that promised much, but which fell apart from early March as they won only two of their last sixteen League matches, ten of which ended in defeat. Latics finished with thirty-eight points, the same total as the previous year, but ended four places higher in thirteenth spot.

Halom was a resounding success, finishing top scorer with twenty-three goals in all competitions, while Hurst had been a calming influence at the back as young players Carl Valentine and Gary Hoolickin also broke into the team.

While average home attendances were 9,998, there was one lucrative pay day when Latics played at Liverpool in the third round of the FA Cup in front of a crowd of 52,455.

The popular Ian Robins was transferred to Bury for £25,000 in the summer of 1977, and was replaced by tough-tackling midfield man Mike Bernard, a £10,000 capture from

THE GOAL THAT NEVER WAS: Ronnie Blair's effort against Manchester United in 1974 hit the back stanchion of the net and bounced back into play. To the astonishment of everybody at Boundary Park, the referee waved play on.

Everton. But the most significant arrival was striker Steve Taylor, ironically a Royton lad, in a £37,000 transfer from Bolton. He certainly hit the ground running, scoring twice on his debut and finished the season as leading scorer with twenty-one goals in all competitions to help Latics finish eighth.

It had been a roller-coaster campaign, as Latics made awful start and were third bottom in mid-November. They then went thirteen League games unbeaten, including a run of seven straight victories, which lifted them to sixth spot. Just as Latics were about to mount a challenge for promotion, the season fell apart. They won only two of their last sixteen League fixtures, hurt by injuries to key players.

Latics were saddened to hear of the sudden death of Grove at the age of twenty-nine, only seven months after he had left to join Blackpool.

Frizzell rejected the offer of a five-year £80,000 contract from Walsall to remain at Boundary Park. Latics gave him a pay rise, but no increase in the length of his contract, which still had two years to run.

After a promising start to the 1978/79 season, it once again fell apart after they failed to win in twelve League matches in a three-month period until mid-March. They also failed to win a home game for almost five months as the threat of relegation loomed. However, Latics rediscovered their form to collect fourteen points from their last nine games (there were only two points for a win in those days), and they finished fourteenth.

There was success in the knockouts as Latics reached the final of the Anglo-Scottish Tournament, losing to Burnley over two legs. They beat Stoke and Leicester to reach the fifth round of the FA Cup, before losing 1-0 at home to Tottenham.

Latics broke both transfer records as they sold exciting young winger Carl Valentine to Canadian team Vancouver Whitecaps for £86,000, while striker Simon Stainrod was bought for £60,000 from Sheffield United. The record sum paid for Stainrod was smashed early in the 1979/80 season, when Frizzell paid Manchester City £200,000 for centre-half Kenny Clements.

Later in the season, they paid Sheffield Wednesday £75,000 for striker Rodger Wylde, £25,000 for Manchester City midfielder Ged Keegan, while Pole Ryszard Kowenicki became their first overseas player after a £12,000 move from Widzew Lodz.

It was also the end of an era as Wood was handed a free transfer after a record 524 League appearances and a total of 570 in all competitions. As for the season, it was one that lacked consistency as Latics finished eleventh, with Stainrod top scorer on eleven goals, closely followed by Jim Steel with ten.

Latics became only the second club in Division Two to install undersoil heating at a cost of £60,000. This was the 'Meltaway' system that came from a Swedish company.

Paul Futcher was the major summer signing in 1980, costing £150,000 from Manchester City, but in November there was an unpopular departure as Stainrod was sold to Queens Park Rangers for a club record £250,000. Latics made a £190,000 profit in only twenty months. The cash was needed as attendances that season plunged to an average of 6,502, though Frizzell invested £70,000 of the money to buy Roger Palmer from Manchester City.

Latics' form was again inconsistent as they finished fifteenth and three points clear of the relegation places, but were only eleven behind promoted Swansea. They did reach an important milestone in the season, though, as a home success against Blackburn Rovers in November was their 1,000th victory in the Football League.

Blair, second only to Wood in the number of appearances made for Latics, was handed a free transfer in the summer of 1981, a surprise as he had been the team's only ever-present.

Chairman Harry Wilde insisted the only way forward for Latics was with a flourishing youth policy and, in 1981/82, the team at the start of the season had an average age of twenty-two years: 'If you can't buy players, which doesn't guarantee success anyway, you have to find and mould them yourself.'

The squad included the likes of John Ryan, Paul Atkinson, Nicky Sinclair, Darron McDonough and Paul Heaton, who were establishing themselves. Latics' young team made a splendid start to the 1981/82 season. This was the campaign when three points were introduced for a win, and in early December they found themselves in second spot, their highest League position since March 1930. They had become the last team in the entire Football League to lose its unbeaten record when they lost 3-1 at Charlton on 20 October.

Latics and Blackburn Rovers also created a piece of history on Boxing Day 1981 – the fixture was switched from Ewood Park to Boundary Park, where there was undersoil heating, when it became clear it was going to become a victim of the freeze.

After the early promise, the season died a death as during a two-month period from mid-February they failed to win in ten League matches, goals dried up and the dream of a return to the top flight disappeared.

Injuries and suspensions decimated the small squad as only nineteen players were used throughout the entire campaign, in which they finished eleventh. By the season's end, more young players like Andy Goram, John Bowden and Dougie Anderson had been blooded. There was also a worrying dip in crowds towards the end of the season, with an attendance of just 2,904 for the next to last home game against Charlton Athletic.

And it was against that backdrop that Frizzell was sacked in June 1982, after twenty-two years as a player and manager, with a statement declaring the club needed a new challenge and to attract fans through the turnstiles.

LATICS TURN TO ROYLE-TY

One month later, thirty-three-year-old Joe Royle, whose distinguished playing career had just ended, was appointed manager from a list of thirty applicants. He later revealed he was not the first choice as former West Brom centre-half John Wile had initially been given the job, only to reject it after failing to agree to a package.

Royle arrived at a time when Latics' finances were dire, and he immediately found himself under pressure to sell players. The situation eased in November when the club's major shareholder J. W. Lees Brewery bought the Boundary Club and Sports Hall, discharged the bank overdraft, loans and other debts and breathed new life into the club.

There was also a change at the top as Harry Wilde resigned after eight years as chairman and thirteen years as a director due to boardroom politics. Ian Stott, a director since 1974, took over the helm.

Royle was forced to essentially work with what he inherited, though he signed midfielder Tony Henry from Bolton Wanderers for £21,000 in March 1983. He had earlier sold Futcher to Derby County for £100,000. His debut season was a success as Latics finished seventh, only nine points behind promoted Leicester. Indeed, with a decent home record they would probably have gone up, as ten draws and three defeats equated to twenty-nine points lost at Boundary Park. The attractive football played won plaudits, and Latics scored sixty-four League goals, Wylde was top scorer for a third successive season, contributing nineteen and Palmer fifteen.

The honeymoon period ended in 1983/84 as Latics finished fourth bottom, only avoiding relegation by five points – their fortunes plummeted in a season when they were ravaged by injury and misfortune. Palmer top scored with fourteen League and Cup goals.

The transfers of Wylde to Sporting Lisbon, Ryan to Newcastle for £235,000 and Atkinson to Watford for £175,000 left a huge hole in the squad and supporters unhappy.

Royle's marquee summer signing was Martin Buchan on a free from Manchester United, while other significant arrivals were Mark Ward from non-League Northwich Victoria for a bargain £10,000 and, late in the season, striker Mike Quinn from Stockport for £52,000.

Latics kicked off the 1984/85 season as the bookmakers' 100/1 outsiders for the Second Division championship and favourites to be relegated. Willie Donachie was the only summer signing, the left-back joining on a free from Burnley.

Despite continued financial worries caused by dwindling attendances (the average tumbled to 4,725), Latics enjoyed an upturn in fortunes to finish fourteenth thanks to the goals of Quinn, who hit twenty-one in League and Cup. There was a £250,000 cash boost following the transfer of seventeen-year-old striker Wayne Harrison to Liverpool after only eight appearances and two goals for Latics.

Latics were on the rise again in 1985/86, despite further major upheavals in the playing squad – Ward was sold to West Ham for £250,000 two days before the start of the campaign, while Quinn left for Portsmouth in March for £150,000. Royle was proving an astute wheeler dealer in the transfer market, paying £15,000 for Barnsley striker Ron Futcher, who was seventeen-goal top scorer in his debut campaign, and £55,000 for Leeds centre-half Andy Linighan.

Young players like Goram and Andy Barlow were established, while Mike Milligan and Gary Williams also emerged. Indeed, Goram won the first of his forty-three caps for Scotland in 1986.

Latics started well and found themselves second in the table in early November. They then lost ten of their next eleven games and drawing the remaining one, to tumble to fifth bottom by the end of the year. Bearing in mind the disastrous spell in which only one point was picked up from a possible thirty, Latics produced a spirited showing in the second half of the season to climb back up the table to finish eighth. Futcher scored in each of the last two games of the season to finish top scorer with seventeen, edging out Palmer, who found the net sixteen times.

The 1986/87 season saw Latics invest £385,000 in a plastic pitch in a partnership with Oldham Leisure Services, as it also entailed community use. This was 8,415 square metres of fibriliated polypropylene, and at the time it was the largest artificial sports surface in Great Britain. The work also enabled Latics to remove more than half of the famous Boundary Park slope as the pitch had been almost 2 metres higher at the Rochdale Road End of the ground.

Royle signed a new three-year contract before the kick-off to a campaign that saw the introduction of the end-of-season play-offs. The top two teams in the division would be promoted automatically instead of three. The third, fourth and fifth sides joined the nineteen clubs from the First Division for the one remaining place in Division One.

Latics finished third, which in any other year would have guaranteed automatic promotion. This time, however, it meant a place in the play-off semi-final and heartbreak as they lost to Leeds on the away-goals rule after it was 2-2 on aggregate over the two legs. It was the closest Latics had come to regaining their top-flight status since they lost it in 1923 and they had never been out of the top three all season.

Royle had earlier raided Leeds again, snapping up full-back Denis Irwin on a free and paying £80,000 for winger Tommy Wright. There was also the midseason capture of Grimsby Town captain Kevin Moore to provide defensive solidity.

Latics had proved themselves to be worthy promotion contenders, and the future looked bright as eight of the players who tackled Leeds in the play-offs were aged twenty-three or under. Though the season finished in despair, it was one of significant progress and was viewed as a launch pad to better things.

Palmer was top scorer with seventeen goals, while Futcher contributed fifteen before a £40,000 move to Bradford City in January. There was clearly a hangover to the previous season's disappointment as Latics finished the 1987/88 season in tenth place. They managed only four League victories by early December from nineteen attempts, losing eleven times.

Above: MIGHTY QUINN: Latics' striker Mick Quinn is beaten to the ball by Manchester City goalkeeper Alex Williams during a Division Two match at Maine Road in 1984.

Right: SEEING RED: A friendly against Manchester United in 1985 as Latics' Tony Henry (*left*) and United's Norman Whiteside do battle.

However, there was then a huge turnabout in their fortunes as they lost only four times in their final twenty-five League matches, in which they defeated the likes of Manchester City, Aston Villa, Middlesbrough, Blackburn Rovers and Crystal Palace.

The team continued to evolve, with striker Andy Ritchie signed from Leeds United for £50,000, while midseason centre-forward Frank Bunn was bought from Hull City for £80,000, and Manchester City reserve defender Earl Barrett captured for £35,000. Ritchie hit the ground running as he and Palmer finished the season joint top scorers with twenty goals apiece. Moore left for Southampton for £125,000 as he had a clause in his contract that allowed him to move if Latics failed to win promotion, while Linighan was sold to Norwich City for a club record £350,000 in March.

The strong finish to the previous season meant that Latics entered the 1988/89 season in fine spirits. Royle hoped it would be a lucky seventh season as manager. It was no longer viewed as a question of Second Division survival.

The season certainly didn't proceed as scripted, as underachieving Latics finished eighteenth following a campaign disrupted by injuries and defensive ills. Goalkeeper Goram was transferred to Hibernian for £325,000 and the departures of Moore and Linighan ripped the heart out of the back line.

Latics scored seventy-five League goals, and that was only bettered by promoted Chelsea and Manchester City, but they conceded seventy-two. Only the bottom two clubs leaked more.

Royle had to rebuild the back line by bringing in goalkeepers Andy Rhodes from Doncaster Rovers for £55,000 and Jon Hallworth, a £75,000 capture from Ipswich Town, along with centre-backs Ian Marshall and Andy Holden from Everton and Wigan Athetic for fees of £100,000 and £130,000 respectively. He also snapped up defender Paul Warhurst from Manchester City for a giveaway £10,000.

Though it was a season of disappointment, Palmer reached a notable milestone when he smashed the club's all-time record for League goals. The first of his brace in a 4-0 win against Ipswich Town took his total to 111 and past the record set thirty-five years earlier by Gemmell. Palmer finished with fifteen goals for the season, one behind Ritchie.

After finishing eighteenth the previous season, Latics kicked off 1989/90 with no great expectations, especially after failing to win any of their first four League games. Nobody could ever have envisaged it would develop into the most successful season in the club's history.

They produced one giant-killing act after another to reach the final of the Littlewoods Cup and a first Wembley appearance in the club's history. They so nearly made it a double, taking Manchester United to a replay in the semi-final of the FA Cup, and they also narrowly missed out on promotion.

Only six survivors remained from the 1987 play-off squad – Irwin, Donachie, Barlow, Palmer, Milligan and Williams – as Royle continually had to rebuild and evolve his squad.

Above: TOP BOSS: Success in 1989/90 for Joe Royle, who won a Barclays Manager of the Month award.

Right: TRICKY RICKY: A spectacular goal celebration from Rick Holden in 1989/90 season.

THE PINCH-ME SEASON

Before the start of the 1989/90 season, Wright was transferred to Leicester for £300,000, while Peter Skipper and John Kelly moved to Walsall for a combined £65,000. Royle hit the jackpot with his signings, notably wingers Neil Adams and Rick Holden, signed from Everton and Watford for fees of £100,000 and £165,000 respectively. Later in the season, he returned to Watford to pay £150,000 for Neil Redfearn, as well as splashing out a then club record £225,000 for Bournemouth striker Paul Moulden.

The Cup adventures began in the Littlewoods Cup as they beat Leeds United home and away. That was followed by a 7-0 home win against Scarborough, who had beaten Chelsea in the previous round. That was the night Frank Bunn scored six goals, which remains a competition record for the number of goals scored in one match.

The football world suddenly began to sit up and take notice of Latics when they defeated reigning First Division champions Arsenal 3-1 on the plastic, and Royle's stock rose as he rejected the chance to manage Manchester City in December 1989, preferring to stay and finish the job he had started.

The giant-killing continued in the Littlewoods Cup as Ritchie's goal deep into stoppage time earned a 2-2 draw at Southampton, who were beaten in the replay, while West Ham were blitzed 6-0 at Boundary Park in the first leg of the semi-final, making the return at Upton Park a formality. Sadly, Latics lost 1-0 to Nottingham Forest at Wembley, where they had a 30,000 following, Oldham becoming a ghost town following an exodus.

Latics were already well on the road to Wembley when they embarked upon their FA Cup campaign as they overcame Birmingham City after a replay, Brighton, Everton following two replays, and Aston Villa to reach the semis, when they were paired with Manchester United. The initial game ended 3-3 after extra time and the two teams returned to Maine Road three days later, where United scraped home 2-1, again after an additional thirty minutes.

Latics played a total of sixty-five competitive games (Barrett played in all sixty-five of them) and simply ran out of steam in the League. They managed only three wins from their last twelve matches to finish eighth in Division Two and only missed out on a play-off place by four points. The exploits of the little club from Lancashire had captured the hearts of the nation, and many adopted them as their second team.

Ritchie had a season to remember with an impressive haul of twenty-eight League and Cup goals, while Palmer contributed twenty. Fans, swept along by the euphoria, ensured crowds at Boundary Park were their highest for more than ten years, averaging 11,240 in League and Cup.

Above: SNOW SCENE: A clearing operation in full swing on the plastic pitch in the winter of 1989/90.

Right: STITCH IN TIME: Andy Ritchie was voted by Latics' fans as the club's greatest-ever player.

Latics were unable to repeat their Cup exploits in 1990/91, but they achieved their goal in regaining their top-flight status after an absence of sixty-eight years. That was achieved despite the loss of two of their most influential players, captain Mike Milligan and the ever-dependable right-back Denis Irwin, as Latics twice broke the club record for a sale.

Manchester United paid an initial £625,000 for Irwin, which would later rise to £700,000, while Milligan went to Everton for £1 million. They were sums of money a club of Latics' size simply could not turn down.

Royle reinvested £1.1 million as he smashed the club record for a purchase three times that summer. Goalkeeper John Keeley, a £240,000 buy from Brighton was followed by £450,000 for Nottingham Forest striker David Currie and £460,000 for Hull City centre-half Richard Jobson.

There was a tidal wave of optimism as the season kicked off as the number of season ticket holders doubled to 5,000 and the club also had the same number of members. It was not misplaced as Latics won 3-2 on the opening day at Wolves, where defender-turned-striker Ian Marshall scored a hat-trick and made a perfect start, winning their first five games which equalled a best previous opening in 1929/30.

Latics stretched their unbeaten run at the start of a season to a club record fourteen League matches, which bettered the previous best of thirteen in 1952/53, when they won the Third Division North title as the omens were looking positive. They extended it to sixteen games – the first defeat was incurred in mid-November, when they lost 1-0 at Port Vale.

Royle reinforced his squad midseason with the acquisitions of Norwegian international Gunnar Halle and Scottish midfielder Paul Kane for a combined £630,000.

There was a brief spell in March/April when Latics looked as though they might blow their promotion hopes after a run of only one win in eight games. However, they overcame that wobble and went to Ipswich Town with four games remaining, knowing that victory would clinch promotion. The 3,000 fans who made the lengthy trip to East Anglia were rewarded as two goals from Marshall secured a 2-1 victory. Latics finished the season in style, being crowned champions on a dramatic day that will never be forgotten.

Second-placed Latics were at home to Sheffield Wednesday, who were third, while leaders West Ham were at home to Notts County, who were fourth. Latics looked to have blown their chances as Wednesday established a 2-0 advantage after almost an hour, even though West Ham were slipping to a 2-1 defeat.

They needed a footballing miracle, which came as Latics launched an unbelievable fight back with goals from Marshall, Paul Bernard, in only his second game, and Neil Redfearn, whose 92nd minute penalty snatched the title by one point. It sparked incredible scenes of celebration at Boundary Park as Latics returned to the top flight for the first time in sixty-eight years. There was embarrassment on the part of the Football League as the trophy, hastily despatched by courier, arrived with West Ham's name engraved on it.

It was a weekend to remember. The next day there was an open-top bus ride from the ground to the Civic Centre for an official reception. On Monday, 15,700 returned to Boundary Park for Palmer's well deserved and earned testimonial against Manchester City. Marshall finished top scorer with eighteen League and Cup goals, followed by Redfearn and Ritchie with seventeen and fifteen respectively. Palmer reached a milestone of 150

CHAMPAGNE MOMENTS: There were celebrations on the flight back from the Littlewoods Cup semi-final at West Ham, where Latics booked their Wembley place. Pictured (*from left*): Paul Warhurst, Nick Henry and Andy Barlow.

CAPTAIN MARVELS: Bryan Robson (*left*) and Mike Milligan line up before the 1990 semi-final of the FA Cup between Latics and Manchester United at Maine Road.

WEMBLEY WAY: Latics' fans on the approach to the stadium before the final of the Littlewoods Cup.

GHOST TOWN: An exodus of 30,000 Latics' fans headed for Wembley, leaving Oldham almost deserted.

ROYLE FAMILY: Fans devised memorable banners for their big day out at Wembley.

Above: PROUD MOMENT: Joe Royle and Brian Clough lead out their teams for the final of the Littlewoods Cup.

Right: ROYLE MEETS ROYAL: Joe Royle is introduced to the Duchess of Kent at Wembley.

goals for Latics with his strike in a 2-2 draw at Swindon. There was also a huge increase in average home League attendances to 13,234.

Royle spent £1.6 million on four major acquisitions for the start of their First Division campaign, including the return of Milligan for a club record £600,000 after his move to Everton didn't work out. There was a second signing from the Toffees as legend Graeme Sharp was bought for £500,000, while Coventry City centre-half Brian Kilcline cost £400,000 and Halifax Town youngster Craig Fleming arrived in an £80,000 deal that later increased to £150,000 through add-ons.

The season began with a new look at Boundary Park where the artificial pitch had gone (it was not allowed in the top division), while the Chaddy End terracing had disappeared to become a new all-seater stand. Latics could not have had a bigger opening game than away to Liverpool, where Barrett gave them the lead before the hosts hit back to win 2-1.

Chelsea were the visitors for Latics' first home match and they recorded their first victory, with Marshall, Rick Holden and Currie scoring in a 3-0 success.

Latics enjoyed some notable triumphs, including winning at Manchester City and at home to champions Leeds United, who had Eric Cantona making his debut that day. Latics they finished seventh in the twenty-two club division, nine points clear of the relegation places. This was achieved despite a crippling injury list and big turnover in the playing staff as Barrett was sold to Aston Villa for £1.7 million, which remains a club record, having been bought for just £35,000. Currie and Kane were allowed to move on after unsuccessful stays. There was one notable arrival, midfield man Neil McDonald, in a £500,000 deal, becoming the fifth former Evertonian to join Latics.

Sharp was top scorer with fifteen League and Cup goals, while home League attendances averaged 15,121, with four topping 18,000 against the two Manchester teams, Liverpool and Leeds.

Above right: LAP OF HONOUR: Latics' players thank the vast travelling army at the end of the game.

Right: COMMEMORATIVE COVER: The Royal Mail produced a commemorative cover to mark Latics' appearance at Wembley.

Below: WEMBLEY ACTION: Latics' captain Mike Milligan and Nottingham Forest's Nigel Clough in a chase for possession.

Above: BOOK LAUNCH: Stewart Beckett signs copies of his book *The Team From a Town of Chimneys* flanked by Latics' legends Ronnie Blair, Earl Barrett, Ian Wood and Roger Palmer.

Left: GOING UP: Ian Marshall celebrates one of his two goals at Ipswich, which clinched promotion back to the top flight after an absence of sixty-eight years.

OOPS: Latics weren't expected to be crowned Second Division champions in 1990/91, and even the Football League had West Ham's name engraved on the trophy.

CELEBRATIONS: The bubbly was flowing in the changing rooms after Latics beat Sheffield Wednesday on the last day of the season to be crowned Second Division champions.

CIVIC PRIDE: Latics had an open-top bus tour of the town to celebrate their promotion to the First Division.

TESTIMONIAL: All-time leading goalscorer Roger Palmer carries son Gavin on to the Boundary Park pitch for his testimonial against Manchester City, two days after Latics clinched the Second Division title.

SIT DOWN: The Chaddy End becomes all-seater in 1991.

PLASTIC PITCH: Latics' artificial pitch had to be replaced by grass in 1991 following their promotion to the First Division.

OFFICIAL TEAM PHOTO: The 1990/91 Second Division championship-winning team.

BACK IN THE BIG TIME

The 1991/92 season marked the dawn of a new era as Latics became founder members of the new FA Premier League, the deal with BSkyB earning Latics £1.3 million in that initial campaign, a far cry from the riches of today.

Latics also completed the biggest transfer deal in the club's history, signing Steve Redmond and Neil Pointon from Manchester City for a combined £1.2 million with the £900,000 rated Rick Holden moving to Maine Road as part of the deal. Royle also paid £700,000, which is still a club record, to Aston Villa for striker Ian Olney. Darren Beckford was also captured later in the season from Norwich for £300,000.

There was also a new look at Boundary Park, where the open terracing on the Rochdale Road Stand had been replaced by a £1.9 million covered all-seater stand with a 4,600 capacity.

Latics kicked off their Premier League campaign with a 1-1 draw at Chelsea, which was followed by a 1-1 home draw against Crystal Palace and 5-3 victory against Nottingham Forest at Boundary Park, picking up five points from their first three games. It was to prove a false dawn as despite beating champions-elect Manchester United, the season would see Latics, become embroiled in a desperate scrap for survival, which became known as their 'Great Escape'.

Latics went into the last week of the season cut adrift and needing a miracle to beat the drop. They needed to win their last three games of the season – they had failed to win three in a row all season – and relied on Crystal Palace slipping up. It looked a highly unlikely scenario.

A miracle happened as Latics won at title-chasing Aston Villa – it was a defeat that handed Manchester United their first championship for twenty-six years – and at home to Liverpool and Southampton as they stayed up on goal difference ahead of Palace, who had been eight points clear of Latics heading into the final week of the season.

The last match against Saints was one that has become folklore. Latics, 4-1 ahead, allowed their opponents to cut the deficit to 4-3. It was a nerve-jangling finish, as underlined by Royle anxiously pacing up and down the steps leading to the changing rooms in the dying minutes.

Olney marked his first season by finishing top scorer with thirteen League and Cup goals, while Adams hit nine, including the winner against Manchester United and also important goals against Everton and QPR. Their total of sixty-three League goals was bettered only by champions Manchester United and Blackburn Rovers, but defensively they had the second worst record, conceding seventy-four. Yet such was the tight nature of the table that Latics were only ten points behind sixth-placed Liverpool.

Latics went into the 1993/94 season inspired by minnows Norwich City finishing third in the table the previous campaign, but after winning only twice in their first sixteen

League fixtures, it soon became apparent they would be involved in another battle to avoid relegation. They were ravaged by injuries, with Olney ruled out for the season as Royle snapped up Bradford City striker Sean McCarthy for £500,000 and Norwegian defender Tore Pedersen, though his loan stay was also cut short by injury.

As Latics embarked upon a run that took them to the semi-finals of the FA Cup, this coincided with fortunes in the League improving as they recorded five wins and three draws from ten games. They defeated Derby County, Stoke City, Barnsley and Bolton en route to a semi-final against Manchester United at Wembley. Latics took the lead in extra time through a goal from Pointon. They were 53 seconds away from reaching the final when Mark Hughes scored a spectacular equaliser. It forced a replay at Maine Road, where Latics were beaten 4-1, after which their season imploded.

Latics failed to win in their last seven League games (the final four were played in eight days due to the Cup run causing a fixture pile up), yet they still went into the final game with a slim hope of surviving. Latics needed to win at Norwich and for Wimbledon to beat Everton to stay up and for the Toffees to be relegated. And there was a time when it looked as though it might happen, when Latics led at Carrow Road and Wimbledon were 2-0 ahead. This was false hope as Norwich equalised and Everton pulled off their own great escape, overturning the deficit to win 3-2. 'Morale-wise, who can say what effect that Mark Hughes goal had on so many people?' Royle added after the Norwich game.

Latics carried out a £450,000 refurbishment of the main stand to extend the roof over the paddock where 900 seats had been installed. Seats were also installed in the Lookers Stand paddock as the ground became a 13,800 all-seat stadium for the 1994/95 season to comply with the Taylor Report, which followed the Hillsborough tragedy five years earlier.

Milligan left for a second time, this time to Norwich for £850,000 while Aberdeen's Lee Richardson was signed as a replacement for £300,000. It was also the end of an era as Palmer left after thirteen-and-a-half years, in which he had scored a total of 156 goals.

Latics retained the nucleus of the squad in a concerted effort to try and immediately regain their Premier League status.

THE GREAT ESCAPE: Latics' players on their lap of honour following their last day 4-3 home win against Southampton in May 1993, which staved off relegation. They beat Aston Villa, Liverpool and Saints in the space of six days to stay up on goal difference ahead of Crystal Palace.

THE END OF THE ROYLE ERA

It soon became apparent this would not happen, and November 1994 marked the end of an era when Royle, whose last buy was Southampton striker Nicky Banger for £250,000, decided to accept an offer to manage Everton, the club he had supported since he was a boy and where he had also been a playing legend.

Royle was succeeded by Sharp, who appointed former Everton manager Colin Harvey as his assistant and the pair guided Latics to fourteenth place. McCarthy finished the season as top scorer with eighteen, while Ritchie reached the milestone of 100 goals for Latics to become third in the all-time list behind Palmer and Gemmell. Ritchie scored thirteen of his 104 goals that season only to be handed a free transfer by Sharp, who also released long-serving Andy Barlow at the end of the season.

The 1995/96 season was one of turmoil for Latics in Division One, as they only narrowly avoided relegation. They only stayed up by a margin of four points thanks to a strong finish to the season in which they picked up ten points from a possible twelve from their final four fixtures to climb out of the bottom three.

Jobson was sold to Leeds for £1 million, and Sharp was able to invest much of that money on striker Stuart Barlow, who was bought from Everton for £450,000 and Toddy Orlygsson from Stoke City for £180,000. But it was a sign of the ever-increasing malaise that average home League attendances were now down to 6,627.

There was to be no escape in 1996/97 as Latics were relegated from Division One, finding themselves in the third tier of English football for the first time since 1973/74. Goalkeeper Paul Gerrard left for Everton in a £1 million deal, Chris Makin moved on a controversial free to French club Olympique Marseille, while in the midseason Gunnar Halle moved to Leeds for £400,000.

Latics made a horrendous start, failing to register their first League victory until 5 October after ten unsuccessful attempts. Sharp brought in reinforcements, including goalkeeper Gary Kelly for a nominal £10,000 from Bury, centre-back Shaun Garnett from Swansea for £150,000, and striker Ian Ormondroyd from Bradford City.

Latics remained in the relegation places for most of the season, and in February 1996 Sharp resigned, citing the club's lack of ambition as the reason for his departure. Neil Warnock was quickly appointed new manager, with Ritchie returning as player-coach, but they were unable to stave off relegation as Latics finished second bottom.

Nick Henry's lengthy association with Latics ended as he was sold by Warnock to Sheffield United in a £500,000 deal, which saw Aussie centre-back Doug Hodgson move to Boundary Park. Warnock also signed Lee Duxbury, Paul Reid and winger Matthew Rush from West Ham for £165,000.

Relegation saw an exodus of players as Fleming was sold to Norwich for £600,000, while senior players like Hallworth, Richardson and Banger all left.

Warnock, who had a great record of guiding teams to promotion, looked as though he was going to add Latics to his impressive CV as they were fourth in the table in mid-February. However, a run of only one win in twelve League games in February/March put paid to their promotion hopes and they finished thirteenth.

Warnock brought in Liverpool legend Bruce Grobbelaar to play the last four games of the season as cover for the injured Kelly. The disappointing finish to the season saw Warnock not offered a new deal and he was replaced by Ritchie, who was a popular choice with the fans.

Ritchie's managerial debut proved a baptism of fire in 1998/99, a campaign in which Latics only avoided relegation to the basement division of English football on the last dramatic day to the season. Latics, who had sold Carl Serrant to Newcastle for £500,000 before the season kicked off, found themselves in the bottom four with one week of the season remaining, but escaped following back-to-back home wins against Stoke and Reading.

Everything hinged on the last day. Had they beaten Reading, Latics would still have gone down if York had overcome Manchester City, who did them a favour posting a 4-0 victory as Latics finished one point clear of the relegated Minstermen.

Ritchie pulled off one master stroke of transfer activity by signing Sheffield Wednesday legend John Sheridan, who had been playing in the Conference with Doncaster after being released by Bolton.

However, striker Steve Whitehall, a £50,000 summer signing from Mansfield, failed to make an impression, and John McGinlay, a vastly experienced front man, had to retire through injury after only five months at the club.

Ritchie's first season was played against a backdrop of unrest off the field, with chairman Ian Stott resigning after sixteen years at the helm after it emerged he had held 'informal' talks with Bury and Rochdale over a possible merger, which was viewed as a possible solution to continuing financial woes. Vice chairman David Brierley moved up, but Mr Stott remained on the board of directors as vice chairman.

On a brighter note, however, Sports Park 2000 received the go-ahead in February 1999 after five years on the drawing board. The project would see a new 15,000-capacity stadium constructed on Clayton Playing Fields with the football pitches transferred to the site of Boundary Park, though there was fierce opposition from the Clayton Action Group.

Latics looked to be in for another long, hard season after losing their first five matches of 1999/2000 and winning only once by the second week of October. Ritchie arrested the slide and Latics finished that campaign in fourteenth place, comfortably clear of the relegation places, which was no mean achievement bearing in mind the lack of financial muscle as fifteen of the twenty-eight players used in the League were home produced.

However, events of that season were completely overshadowed by events off the pitch as major shareholder J. W. Lees, who held a 48 per cent stake, put the club up for sale in June 1999. Directors David Brierley, Peter Chadwick and Derek Taylor bought the club, but within weeks Boundary Park was sold to Hiretarget for £3 million. Hiretarget was a joint venture company between Oldham Council and Brookhouse Developments, which was involved in the building of Sports Park 2000.

Latics' debts had reached crisis point at £2.7 million. with a quote at the time saying the club was on the brink of oblivion. A deal saw Hiretarget lease Boundary Park back to the football club. Latics' owners only viewed this as a short-term measure and the club needed future investment, which is why they decided the time was right to sell.

Leeds Sporting plc, which owned Leeds United, bought a 9.9 per cent stake in Latics in what was viewed as forming a future link to benefit both clubs. But that encouraging news was soured when Latics learned that Sports Park 2000 appeared doomed as Cllr Richard Knowles vowed to protect the land left in trust to the town by Ina Clayton.

Latics made another awful start to the season in 2000/01, which mirrored the previous year. They won only one of their first eleven League matches, finding themselves in the relegation places for most of the opening three months of the campaign.

The signings of David Eyres and Tony Carrs on the same day in October helped spark the revival as Latics recovered well to eventually finish fifteenth. They had been four places higher before losing their last two matches.

Latics finally thought they had banished their money troubles for good in May 2001 when successful businessman Chris Moore (executive chairman of computer systems company Torex plc, a company with an annual turnover of £350 million) completed a takeover and vowed he would lead the club back to the Premier League within five years. Mr Moore immediately invested £1.5 million, which was part of the agreement to take a majority shareholding.

Though Latics' fortunes initially improved, Mr Moore's reign ended less than two years later, he left the club on the verge of extinction, a result of his extravagant spending. with the club losing a mind-blowing £50,000 each week.

Ritchie had his contract terminated by Mr Moore in October 2001 after he refused a place on the board as technical director, as the owner wanted to put in place a new management structure. Ironically, it came after Latics' best start to a season for twelve years, as they had been top of the table in mid-September and in eighth place at the time of his dismissal, days after Ritchie had paid £200,000 for Bury full-back Chris Armstrong.

Mick Wadsworth was appointed the new manager in early November, with Iain Dowie arriving as his number two, and the pair guided the club to a ninth-place finish, despite losing 7-1 to Cardiff City in March, a club record home defeat.

Whereas Ritchie had managed on a shoestring throughout most of his time as manager, Wadsworth was able to spend freely, building a completely new side and splashing out £225,000, the club's highest fee for four years, for Watford striker Allan Smart. Wadsworth also bought Newcastle centre-half David Beharall, and £150,000 also signed the likes of Fitz Hall, Dean Holden, Julian Baudet, Paul Muray, David Reeves, Matty Appleby and Michael Clegg, while Andy Goram, almost thirty-eight years of age, returned to play four games as Latics were short of goalkeeping cover.

There was a turbulent finish to the season when Smart, signed six months earlier, was sacked after being charged with assault and a public order offence. The striker was already on bail for a similar offence. Wadsworth's stay was equally short as he, too, left after only

OWNER: The controversial Chris Moore presents Lee Duxbury with a player of the year award.

six months following a row with Mr Moore, who had proposed to make cuts to the club's youth programme.

Dowie was promoted to manager and made some high-profile signings for 2002/03, including the loan capture of Argentinian under-20 and under-23 international Cristian Colusso, a midfielder who was valued at £2 million by his club Rosario Central. He also brought in free agent striker Clyde Wijnhard, who once cost Leeds United £1.5 million, and Manchester City front man Chris Killen for £250,000, along with Wayne Andrews, a highly rated striker from non-League Chesham.

It was a remarkable first season for Dowie as Latics qualified for the promotion play-offs, where they lost 2-1 on aggregate to QPR in the two-legged semi-final. Latics had been top of the table in early October and found themselves in the play-off places from mid-September onwards. They only missed out on automatic promotion by four points.

There was also a run to the fourth round of the Worthington Cup after wins at Derby and West Ham in the two previous rounds with David Eyres, who was in his fortieth year, enjoying a season to remember, finishing as sixteen-goal top scorer. This success was achieved against a backdrop of a new financial crisis, as it was revealed Latics were facing the gravest crisis in the club's history.

As the club was expected to lose £2.6 million in the current trading year (the deficit had trebled under Mr Moore), in October the club called in business recovery group BDO Stoy Hayward after Mr Moore, who had pumped in £3.6 million in his seventeen months as owner, revealed he couldn't fund them more than halfway through the current campaign. A £1 million appeal was immediately launched, and Mr Moore promised to match it if the target was met. He also vowed not to walk out, but in March 2003 he quit the board to become honorary joint president, though he retained his majority holding in the club.

The summer of 2003 saw Mr Moore preside over a fire sale of the best players, including Fitz Hall, Chris Armstrong and Clint Hill, which raised £500,000. The likes of Carlo Corazzin, Wayne Andrews, Tony Carrs, Josh Low and Duxbury also left. After a buyout by a Norwegian businessman collapsed, Mr Moore sold his 95 per cent stake in the club for £1 to the club's marketing manager, Sean Jarvis, and accountant, Neil Joy, who held the shares on behalf of a potential management buyout.

Latics, who were £2.8 million in debt, had no option but to seek a High Court order, which was granted on 19 August to place the club into administration, with insolvency experts PFK appointed to run the club.

THREE AMIGOS BECOME SAVIOURS

Latics began the 2003/04 season with a side that scarcely resembled the one from the previous campaign, as Dowie was forced into emergency signings of little-known players while also turning to youth-team players simply to field a team.

Luckily, Latics found saviours in the form of New York-based businessmen Simon Blitz, Danny Gazal and Simon Corney – the 'Three Amigos', as they were to become known. In February 2004, they completed the buyout, which had already cost them £7 million, including purchasing the ground and 20-acre site for £4.6 million from the Oldham Council-backed Oldham Property Partnerships. They had been paying the wages for the six preceding months while their takeover was being concluded to keep the club afloat.

They marked their official takeover with 'Celebration Sunday', giving free admission to the home game against Grimsby Town. A capacity crowd of 13,007 turned out, with many locked out and missing a memorable 6-0 victory. The uncertainty had led to Dowie accepting an offer in December to manage Crystal Palace. Messrs Blitz, Gazal and Corney made former Ipswich Town, Arsenal and England midfielder Brian Talbot their first managerial appointment in March 2004.

Despite the massive upheavals, Latics finished fifteenth and avoided meltdown, both on and off the pitch, with home-grown striker Scott Vernon top scorer, scoring fourteen League and Cup goals.

The 2004/05 season was a roller coaster. From the high of beating Manchester City in the third round of the FA Cup and reaching the Northern Area Final of the LDV Vans Trophy, Latics then found themselves fighing to avoid relegation on the last day of the season after Ronnie Moore had replaced Talbot, who was manager for less than one year. Talbot, who made high-profile loan signings including Lee Croft, Neil Kilkenny and Mark Hughes, paid the price as Latics lost all six League games in February. But it was Moore's inspired loan capture of Luke Beckett, with six goals in the last nine games of the season, that proved the key to Latics staying up.

It was a close shave as Latics, Milton Keynes Dons and Torquay were all battling on the last day of the season to keep clear of the fourth and final relegation place. Latics had to beat Bradford City, which they did 2-1 with goals from Killen and Beckett, and they stayed up by just one point. MK Dons were also victors, but Torquay were demoted after losing at Colchester.

Off the field, the owners revealed plans to quit Boundary Park to build a new stadium at Ferney Field Farm, Chadderton, though this was shelved eight months later when farmer John Blakeman refused to sell his land.

THE THREE AMIGOS: Danny Gazal (*left*), Simon Corney (*centre*) and Simon Blitz, who completed a takeover in 2004.

Above left: GREAT SCOTT: Scott Vernon celebrates his match-winning goal against Manchester City.

Above right: CELEBRATIONS: The jubilant scenes in the dressing room following the victory against Manchester City.

In February 2006, Latics revealed an ambitious £80 million redevelopment for Boundary Park, which involved a new stand to raise capacity to 16,000 along with housing and commercial partnerships.

The 2005/06 season showed a marked improvement under Moore as Latics finished tenth and had been on the fringe of the play-offs until early April. They failed to win any of their last seven League games, and finished six points shy of the play-offs.

Beckett returned for a second loan spell from Sheffield United and was eighteen-goal top scorer, while Moore also brought in the likes of Chris Porter, Paul Warne, Andy Liddell and Richie Wellens. It was also the season local lad Chris Taylor made his bow.

Moore had never been fully accepted by supporters and the owners bowed to pressure, Moore losing his job despite a top-half finish. John Sheridan, the Sheffield Wednesday legend who had joined Latics as a player in 1998 before having various roles on the backroom staff, was elevated to the manager's job.

It was a debut season to remember for Sheridan in 2006/07 as Latics reached the Division One play-offs, where they lost 5-2 on aggregate to Blackpool in the two-legged semi-final. Latics had been top of the table in early February, but then lost four games in a row and had to settle for sixth spot and the last play-off place.

Sheridan's key signing was Leeds United centre-back Sean Gregan, following a successful loan spell, while Porter was the leading scorer with twenty-two League and Cup goals. After eighteen months of work and consultations, Latics submitted a planning application for the Oldham Arena at Boundary Park, though, sadly, it would never see light of day due to the economic crash.

There was controversy early in the 2007/08 season when Latics signed former Premier League striker Lee Hughes on his release from prison, having served three years of a six-year sentence after being convicted of causing death by dangerous driving. Hughes formed a new strike partnership with Craig Davies, who was signed from Wolves for £65,000, as the pair helped offset the loss of Porter to Motherwell. Latics, who had rejected offers for Porter, were unhappy with how he left as a free agent with no recompense, as his move was to Scotland, which is a different UEFA member.

Latics recovered from a disappointing start to the season (they were in the relegation places in late October) to finish eighth, though the play-offs were always out of reach as

MANAGERS REUNITED: Joe Royle, Bill Urmson, who was Andy Ritchie's number two, Graeme Sharp and Jimmy Frizzell.

CENTENARY: Stewart Beckett produced this impressive team photo to mark the club's 100th anniversary.

CITY BEATEN: Latics' Will Haining and Manchester City's Sylvan Distin lead out the teams at Boundary Park before their FA Cup tie in 2005.

OFF THE MARK: Chris Taylor celebrates the first goal of his career at Boundary Park against Doncaster Rovers in March 2007.

they finished nine points adrift of the top six. There was also the joy of another FA Cup upset, as Gary McDonald's spectacular winner gave Latics a 1-0 third-round victory at Everton.

Latics had another managerial change in 2008/09 when the season unravelled after trouble flared following the now infamous night out at the dogs at Belle Vue greyhounds. Sheridan, whose side had been in the promotion play-off places until early March, lost his job following a 6-2 defeat at Milton Keynes Dons, and Joe Royle made a triumphant return as caretaker manager until the end of the season.

Latics went eleven League games without a win in March/April under Sheridan, but Royle still managed to finish tenth in a campaign that saw Hughes finish top scorer with eighteen League goals. Dave Penney, who had an impressive CV at Doncaster and Darlington, was appointed manager with Latics, hoping he would emulate previous successes.

Latics revealed plans for another move from Boundary Park. This time they were planning to relocate to the Lancaster Club, Broadway, though this too would later flounder and be abandoned due to planning issues.

It turned out a disappointing campaign in 2009/10 as Latics finished sixteenth and crashed out of all three cup competitions in the first round. The football under Penney failed to inspire, as did his moves in the transfer market, where the £50,000 capture of Glasgow Rangers' midfielder Dean Furman was probably the one exception.

SUPER MAC: Gary McDonald after scoring for Latics in their FA Cup tie at Everton in 2008.

PAYING HOMAGE: Chris Taylor pays homage to the boot that scored Latics' match-winning goal at Everton.

Above: SHEZ SALUTE: Manager John Sheridan at the end of the Cup tie at Everton, where Latics won 1-0.

Right: CELEBRATION: Lee Hughes' familiar goalscoring jig.

The unpopular Penney was removed with twelve months of his contract remaining and replaced by fiery Scot Paul Dickov, who Latics provided with an opening into management. Dickov's passion lifted Latics, who were in the play-off places in mid-February before their season fell apart spectacularly. They failed to win in twelve League games, and recorded one win in seventeen as they eventually finished seventeenth.

Latics had another disappointing campaign in 2011/12 as they finished sixteenth following another wretched run late in the campaign. This time they recorded two wins in fourteen games. The only cheer came in the FA Cup, when Latics were drawn in the third round at Liverpool, where Robbie Simpson's spectacular strike gave them the lead before they eventually lost 5-1.

Latics also reached the Northern Area final of the Johnstone's Paint Trophy, where there was heartbreak as they lost 3-1 over the two legs to Chesterfield.

Dickov failed to complete a third season, as he lost his job in February 2013, ironically only one week after his side had beaten Liverpool 3-2 at Boundary Park in one of the biggest FA Cup upsets for many years. Latics' joy in the FA Cup – they had won at the Championship club in the third round – bought Dickov time as their League form was awful and they had become embroiled in a scrap against relegation, despite the goals of Jose Baxter, the former Everton striker who was their marquee signing.

Baxter had been tipped for stardom at Everton but rejected the offer of a new two-year contract at the age of twenty to pursue of first-team football. After a move to Crystal Palace failed to materialise, Dickov pulled off a coup by persuading him to join Latics.

Head of Youth Tony Philliskirk was placed in control of the first team for the fifth-round tie against Everton, when Matt Smith, who had scored twice against Liverpool, netted an equaliser deep into stoppage time. This forced a replay, which Latics lost 3-1.

Latics appointed Lee Johnson in March 2013 and, at the age of thirty-one, he became the youngest manager in the club's history. It was a tough start for Johnson, as Latics avoided relegation by only three points. The three wins recorded in the space of one week in April against Bury, Yeovil and Crawley were hugely important, and Smith scored in each of them.

There was incredible hype surrounding the Yeovil game as it pitted father against son when Lee was up against his dad Gary. It was the first time this had happened since the early 1970s, when Bill Dodgin and Bill Dodgin junior were managerial adversaries.

Johnson's first full season as manager in 2013/14 saw Latics finish fifteenth, though it had been another challenging campaign. Latics, who incredibly drew Liverpool for a third successive season in the FA Cup, found themselves in a battle against relegation. However, an excellent end to the season saw Latics put together a ten-match unbeaten run.

It had been difficult for Johnson; two of his jewels were sold as Baxter joined Sheffield United and James Tarkowski joined Brentford. Though the sums were never disclosed, it is believed the combined fees were in the region of £800,000.

So, what does the future hold for Latics, the longest-serving club in the third tier of English football, having remained there since 1997?

There was a new look to Boundary Park for the start of the 2014/15 season as the new £6.5 million North Stand was starting to take shape. It replaced the Broadway Stand, which was demolished in 2008, leaving a three-sided ground.

There was further good news when Latics signed a club record £1 million five-year sponsorship deal with retail giants Sports Direct. Part of the package involved the renaming of Boundary Park, which became SportsDirect.com Park, something which was not universally popular amongst fans.

Latics are hoping the positive vibes from the new stand and the record-breaking sponsorship deal will provide a feel-good factor and herald the start of better times in what has been a challenging period in the club's history.

SCOTS IN BATTLE: Rival managers Kenny Dalglish and Paul Dickov on the touchline at Anfield.

MAGICAL MATT: Big Matt Smith scores for Latics in the FA Cup upset against Liverpool at Boundary Park.

BREAKING: Latics' right-back Connor Brown gets forward against Everton's Steven Pienaar during the FA Cup tie at Boundary Park.

EMOTIONS: Latics' captain Dean Furman's joy is clear to see after Matt Smith's injury-time equaliser earned Latics a 2-2 draw against Everton at Boundary Park.

FLYING HIGH: Matt Smith heads Latics' goal in the FA Cup replay at Everton.

WING WIZARD: Latics' Lee Croft gives Everton defender Sylvan Distin a torrid time.

FLYING FINN: Shefki Kuqi with his spectacular goal celebration.

Right: YOUNG GUN: Lee Johnson became the youngest manager in Latics' history after being appointed at the age of thirty-one.

Below: TACKLE: Liverpool captain Steven Gerrard tries to dispossess Jose Baxter during the FA Cup tie at Boundary Park in 2013.

SIMPSON STUNNER: Robbie Simpson shocks Liverpool by giving Latics the lead at Anfield.

MAN IN THE MASK: James Wesolowski wears a mask in the 2014 FA Cup tie at Liverpool to protect a facial injury.

Above: HEAD TO HEAD: Latics'
Jonson Clarke-Harris and Steven
Gerrard in a duel in the 2014 FA
Cup tie at Liverpool.

Right: JOSE BAXTER BABY: The
former Everton striker celebrates
another goal for Latics.

Above: NEW ERA: The new North Stand at Boundary Park takes shape during the spring of 2014.

Left: JOURNEY'S END: The sun sets over Boundary Park.